The Heart of a Teacher

Blurring Color Lines

DIANA HILTON

authorHOUSE®

AuthorHouse™
1663 Liberty Drive
Bloomington, IN 47403
www.authorhouse.com
Phone: 1-800-839-8640

First published by AuthorHouse 11/23/2010

ISBN: 978-1-4490-5117-4 (sc)
ISBN: 978-1-4490-5118-1 (e)

Printed in the United States of America

Certain stock imagery © Thinkstock.

This book is printed on acid-free paper.

Dedication

I dedicate this book to all of the highly professional, deeply caring, and wonderfully prepared teachers and administrators with whom I have had the privilege to work over my many years of teaching. I also cherish the love and encouragement given me by my husband and children throughout my career. As my grandchildren thrive in school, I know that our system is alive and well. I salute all of those teachers who strive constantly to improve their skills.

Table of Contents

Introduction

This is a story of a year in an elementary school in the inner city. It is a fictionalized account of a teacher's real-life experiences, based on the author's teaching experience with inner-city fifth graders in the early 1990's.

The style of this book is unique, because as the author tells the story, she uses research and comments from reputable authorities to support her observations. These observations are useful in our attempt to improve academic achievement.

The author shows how important every year of a child's life is to his or her overall well-being and academic progress.

During her career, she has used all the teaching techniques she highlights. She introduces and demonstrates a strong set of teaching skills that are often innovative and stimulating.

Everyone interested in education will want to read this story. It will reignite a desire to improve life for all children and get a better understanding of the problems we face in doing so. Teaching is an art, and it is a most challenging profession. Many student teachers and first year staff members comment that teaching is so incredibly hard—harder than they ever dreamed it would be. Teachers work hard and care deeply for each child in each classroom across our nation. The author feels privileged to be a part of such a noble profession that is so important to the next generation.

Prologue

Becoming a Teacher

What helps decide a career path? At age seventeen, I didn't know what I wanted to be. I had no other aim than to go straight to college after graduating from high school. My family had no money, so I had worked as many hours as possible, saving so that I could attend a nearby college.

Part of my resolve stemmed from having a mother who never had the opportunity that I was facing. Her father had been a strict disciplinarian, an Iowa farmer who at the last minute decided he wouldn't finance the college education that his daughter dreamed of having, despite having the means to do so. He walked into her room as she was packing to leave for the University of Iowa and told her the news in the fall of 1927. The announcement changed the course of her life; instead of pursuing further education, she instead found employment in Chicago.

Women didn't have the opportunities then that they do now, and the only job my mother could obtain was as a shopgirl in a jewelry store. When the Great Depression hit in October of 1929, she joined the ranks of the unemployed. Standing in bread lines became a necessity until the economy began to improve and she found a position in a small drug store where she met my father, a pharmacist. He was one of nine children of parents who had emigrated from Ireland; their parties every weekend foreshadowed my mother's eventual future.

Growing up wasn't easy in my life, either. My father gradually worked his way to being a full-fledged alcoholic, and we moved many times as I was growing up. We had very little money; survival was our mode. My mother, however, was a stable force; she worked when she could, but sadly never made enough to support four children. Still, we never took welfare—my mother made sure of that.

When we moved to a small town in Montana, my mother was able to find housing for us by starting a nursing home for the elderly. She lived in a small house with the elderly couple who owned the property and cared for patients, and we all helped as much as we could. My father served as the handyman and lived with the children in a larger home right next door. Both properties were leased to us as long as my mother took care of the owners, who had become too infirm to care for themselves. Their children had hired us and we all felt responsible for their wellbeing.

My father was making an attempt to stop drinking. However, since he had graduated with a degree in pharmaceutical medicine, he had access to ordering drugs for himself under the guise of the nursing home contract. He was a drug addict before it was so prevalent in the United States, and he became totally dependent on the drugs he ordered. If they were late coming by mail, we knew, because he was cranky and unapproachable. Life was hard for my sister and me, because we were teenagers at the time of this transition. Our brother and younger sister were eight and ten years younger than I and weren't as aware of the problems in our family.

What happened to my dad was a result of alcohol, the drugs he took, and a sad incident one cold, wintry night in Montana. My father had installed a floor furnace, and unbeknownst to us, he had vented it improperly. Below-zero temperatures and high winds forced carbon monoxide fumes into our house. The next morning, a Saturday, my mother came over to find out why no one had come over to the nursing home for breakfast. She discovered all of us in our beds, unconscious.

My mother shouted at us to wake up; I remember feeling like her voice was coming through a tunnel from very far away. She threw open the windows, even though they were frozen and hard to move; doing so probably saved us. My father's room was right next to the furnace, so he was worse off than the rest of us, who were upstairs. He was rushed to the hospital by ambulance. My sister was treated next, since her room had a furnace vent in it. My brother and sister had been asleep in the adjoining room, and I lived in the third bedroom upstairs. We regained consciousness rather quickly, because the fumes had reached us last.

My father came home soon from the hospital, but was never quite the same mentally and physically. He became obsessed with entering the nursing home late at night to find people he thought were under the beds, which frightened the patients. He threatened my mother as well, so she was forced to have him removed from our house. He was admitted to a mental institution for help. This was in the mid-1950's. When the movie *One Flew Over the Cuckoo's Nest* came out, I couldn't watch it; it was too real for me, as the shock treatments and forced medications portrayed on the screen actually happened to my father. He came home for a while, but he was basically reduced to a vegetable, and he died at the young age of fifty-two.

At that time, I was only sixteen, but I decided that I had

to be in charge of my life. I knew that hard work was the key to survival, so I worked my way through high school and college. I cleaned the post office and the theatre, and worked as a waitress at the restaurant at the entrance to Yellowstone Park in the summers. I did what I could to support myself even while my mother labored day and night to keep us all together. She wasn't able to make enough for any frills: we wore hand-me-downs and paid for our own dental work, if it was needed.

However, I never considered leaving school to get a full-time job. I was a good student in my small class, and I loved school, studying avidly. I realized early on that education was important, and the seed was planted for me to instill the love of learning into the lives of children.

In an alcoholic family there is always a pleaser—someone who tries to smooth things over, protect others, and empathizes greatly with people in general. I was that person. During college, I began to feel a yearning to support and teach children. I stepped into a classroom and was immediately consumed by my earnest longing to help each student. I have sought to improve the techniques and expertise needed to do so throughout my career. Every year spent teaching had a steep learning curve, but I worked as hard always as I had worked in school in order to better myself as a teacher.

Most of my early experience was in middle-class, mainly white communities. When my husband's job brought us closer to the inner city, I felt a real yearning to encourage children who, perhaps, had life experiences similar to mine. Little did I know what a challenge I faced—and perhaps those challenges will inspire those who have chosen to read my story.

When a teacher retires from teaching, does her experience just fade away? I wondered, as I neared that decisive time in my life. How could I leave a legacy to the profession that I loved and the children I served? It has taken me quite a while to write my book. I humbly present what happened in that year of my life, and in the process, I also share a composite of my years of experience, highlighting techniques that I found to be important in helping children achieve success. I wanted to share the kind of love that comes from the heart of a teacher. I am grateful to those who have chosen to read my story.

Chapter One

The Beginning

It was the beginning of August and I was headed into the inner city for an interview to teach in an impoverished neighborhood. I was not familiar with that part of town, and I found myself lost in a predominantly African-American community. The lone person in view frowned as I approached for directions. He pointed vaguely toward the school and then turned away abruptly. My "Thank you" sounded hollow, bouncing off the back of a seemingly hostile man. My foray into this place might be even harder than my anxious mind had predicted. It was obvious I represented an intrusion to this young man. Would I seem an intrusion to many others in this community? My stomach tied itself into a strange knot that wouldn't dissipate for a while.

A couple of lucky turns brought me to the entrance of the elementary school. The Rosa Parks School sat in the middle of a pretty depressed area of the city. Houses had probably been built in the 1940s or so, and needed some repair; to my eye, the whole neighborhood appeared unloved. The school's parking lot had been newly paved, so it stood out as a welcome freshness, heralding a smooth

1

start for a new school year, and the school building had a well-maintained brick facade and clean windows. I saw the contrast between the brightness of the school and the dullness of the neighborhood as a metaphor for the comparison of life with and without an education.

I had a few minutes to wait for my interview, so I sat and reflected on what had brought me to this moment. My husband of many years and I both worked as educators, he as an administrator and I as a teacher. I had taught all grade levels at some time in my career and had enjoyed the upper elementary levels most recently. Hence, I was applying to teach fifth grade.

Most of my recent experience was in white communities or with about a 70% white and 30% Hispanic mix. I had found that combination could merge the cultures with some success, although there were still color lines. We integrated, as much as possible, but then the children would run from the building at recess and say, "It's us Mexicans against the white guys!" I wanted those color lines to dissolve. I don't mean to imply that we should lose the unique aspects that bring vibrancy to each different society; I have always felt proud to have our country succeed as a "melting pot" of various cultures. Sadly, the nation does not always succeed in this. We have separated neighborhoods of separate cultures far too often, and the community I was entering seemed to be a prime example of that. The school was 95% African American. I was unsure of the makeup of the remainder. I would soon find out how very difficult it was for children inadvertently placed into a different, dominant racial culture.

My husband had been an administrator in a small community for close to twenty years and decided to move around the state to get other experiences before he retired. He currently had accepted a position within driving range of the city. My job searches followed his career, so that was my quest this morning. Climbing out of the car, I peered around the sides of the school. It was so quiet; there were no children around the perimeter. The office door was to the right of the main entrance; I walked in with a sense of entering a new world, of stepping into a new culture.

The office staff ignored me at first. I knew the weeks before school were a frantic attempt to squeeze all the preparations into one short month. There were three ladies busily going about their paperwork. Two were African-Americans (the phrase most used at the time). The third was a Caucasian woman. She pointed to a chair and said it would be a few minutes. I looked around, feeling I was in familiar territory. The copy room to the left and the principal's office to the right set the stage, and I began to feel at home, despite the newness. The floor was shiny and inviting—a fact I loved about schools in August. Soon the scuffmarks of many children would initiate a new year.

The office door opened and a white principal, Ms. Lanikin, and the black head teacher, Jerome, invited me inside. Ms. Lanikin, a middle-aged lady, wore a white blouse and khaki pencil skirt. She appeared to me to be a Type A personality, as she darted from one subject to the other. She was very serious and conducted the entire interview without smiling. Jerome, on the other hand, appeared to be laid back and thoughtful. His hair was shoulder length and he had a nice smile; he seemed to know the right questions to ask me. Both of them were welcoming and interested.

The interview didn't take long. My experience and references were impressive to them, and I answered the barrage of questions easily. They were happy to have an experienced teacher, as most often the new teachers to the district were sent to the inner-city schools. They later wished to transfer as soon as they could due to the difficulty of working with the underprivileged children. Learning this made me feel sad, as I knew that more experienced teachers might deal more effectively with difficult children.[1]

They took me on a tour of the school. I was to be in a doublewide manufactured home that held two classrooms, both fifth grades. The room was so sad, it seemed. It was pretty typical of many classrooms, I suppose, but it seemed smaller and darker than most. The desks were old and used with many scratches on top. The blackboard was green and small. There was a set of windows at the front of the building and one at the back. The back faced a fence and the windows let in very little light. Both sets of windows had dark shades on them, making the whole effect that of a cave. The only equipment was a computer. The textbooks were in cupboards to the back of the room. Other supplies would be available to me, I was assured. I had never been in an outside classroom and wasn't sure I would feel a part of the school as a result, but I took the keys willingly and arranged to return sooner than in-service began to prepare my room. I wished that I would have time to paint it a brighter color.

The other fifth-grade teacher was in her first year, young and inexperienced. She was to occupy the room next to mine. We both faced a daunting challenge: not only were our students of a different race, but they were also from very low-income families. Their struggles were soon to be ours.

---

1   "Reflecting on Longevity, Perimeter Primate.perimeterprimate. blogspot.com/2009/01/call for longevity.

Chapter Two

Meeting the Staff

I entered the library for the first meeting of the year and found a mosaic of black faces and white ones. Many of the teachers had been there for about two or three years. There were several African-American teachers' aides, but I didn't get to visit with them, as they were assigned to the lower grades. The school comprised kindergarten through fifth grade; the only new staff members were myself and the other fifth grade teacher.

There were only three male staff members. There was Jerome, the head teacher; the child development counselor; and the P.E. teacher, who was a huge African-American man. He barely looked at me as I was introduced, and I felt reduced to a non-entity. I was ultra-sensitive, I suppose, about my place on this faculty. Bill certainly looked the part of the stereotypical P.E. teacher. Sweats, a t-shirt, and a whistle rounded out his attire. I knew he was probably very popular with the students and I hoped he would become my friend. However, he showed no interest in getting acquainted.

Bill announced that he would be handing out the equipment for our rooms that day. I expected to receive some playground equipment to be used at recess time, and I figured that when he brought the equipment to me, we could begin the process of getting acquainted. He never came. As timid as I felt in my new environment, I decided not to approach him about it and instead purchased my own equipment. In fact, I bought a lot of supplies on my own, just to be sure I had enough of everything that was needed for my first few weeks of school.

This was not an unusual practice of mine, as the schools where I worked seemed never to have enough supplies. Some children brought their own supplies, but many brought nothing. Most teachers I worked with spent a lot of out-of-pocket money. I took a survey once to find out how much teachers spend out-of-pocket, and discovered it was in the thousands.

The staff meeting was like any other back-to-school gathering. No one seemed to have time to talk. I felt a bit isolated; after all, it is never easy to walk into a new environment. I had done it four or five times prior to this school, so it should have been easy for me, but it wasn't. Entering a new school meant entering a new culture. Much carried over from one school to the next, but you always had to prove yourself again.

I analyzed the environment and knew that it wasn't a completely accepting one. In most schools I had worked in, the veteran teachers took newcomers under their wings and seemed to be willing to share ideas and support. It seemed to me that the healthier the environment, the more the teachers shared. [2] By healthy, I mean that the teachers themselves were well adjusted; they didn't worry about keeping their ideas to themselves, because they cared about the whole

---

2 Little, Judith Warren. "Norms of Collegiality and Experimentation: Workplace conditions of School Success!" http://aer.sage.pub.com/cgi/content/short/19/3/325.

school. Here it seemed so quiet, no one was out in the halls laughing and sharing. I felt lonely.

Later that day, I dropped into Julissa's classroom to get a sense of how discipline was generally handled in most classes. We talked about how the children responded to any type of guidance. Julissa, who had been in the community a long time, looked at me pointedly and said, "We're not suppose to spank, but I get written permission from the mammas to let me, if their child needs it." *Oh*, I thought, despondently. I respected her thoughts, as she knew this community well, but there was no way I could use that approach.[3]

The African-American community in this neighborhood was matriarchal—mainly because most of the fathers were not present. Many families had single moms who struggled to keep their families together when the fathers were in prison, or otherwise not connected to their family. In other families, the grandparents were raising the children. I knew that despite the environment the children were used to, I had to function the way I always did, using my own personality.

Discipline has to come from your own comfort zone and temperament. I am naturally soft-spoken; my approach was to help children manage themselves. I gave firm limits, always searching for that inner self-control that children need to develop to be good citizens. I hoped my approach would be successful in this world.

I believed in using natural consequences as much as possible in the classroom. This prepares children for the real world and is advised by many experts in the field of discipline. For example, if a child went over her allotted time on the computer, than she would to lose her normal

---

3   Park, Alice. "The Long-Term Effects of Spanking," Times Magazine, May3, 2010.

time for a day. If a child lost a book, he needed to replace it by earning the money to do so. If two children didn't play fairly in a game, they should be removed from that game for a period of time. Many experts have advanced this method over the years; it appears to remain an effective system. [4]

I wanted to present an air of compassionate confidence on the first day, so I knew I would be shopping for the first day of school. Clothes are important to me, and I was certain that I needed a proper wardrobe for this school year. That meant a new dress for the first day of school. I spent the Saturday before school started in a quest for that important outfit. After looking in a few stores, I spied the exact dress I wanted. It was blue and gold, with big shiny buttons. It fit perfectly, and I walked out with my first day's outfit in a bag. My husband, who knows me well, smiled at my speed. He doesn't like to shop but is always willing to take me. He either reads his book, or sits and visits with all the other men on benches awaiting their spouses.

For some reason a new dress helps my confidence, so I felt ready and eager, at least for the weekend. As we were driving home from shopping, I thought about the changes in the dress of teachers over time. I could remember when we were never allowed to wear pants to school. Then gradually we were allowed a casual Friday look, and finally anytime we wanted to wear pants we were on our own in decision-making about our individual dressing style. Often teachers wear pants, as they bend frequently to help a child and it is very important to feel comfortable. However, I love to dress up, and so doing so always made me feel ready for the day ahead.

However, on the day before school began, I was nervous

---

4   Turecki, M.D.;Leslie Toner. "The Difficult Child. www. enotaalone.com "Keep Kids Healthy. Discipline Techniques. Keepkidshealthy.com

and anxious for what was sure to be a new adventure, despite all my experience. The rain and the clouds made life seem gloomy that Monday, but the forecast for the next day was not for rain. A touch of luck and a lot of preparation would help the first day go smoothly.

Chapter Three

A Day to Remember

It was the first day of school. I had planned my room, my day, wardrobe and every move I wanted to make. I knew I could do this and still have a flexible approach to the events of the day. Today was the most important opportunity to establish a good impression that would last for the rest of the year. Setting the rules and getting acquainted with my students would make for a full day.

I looked out at the playground from the stoop that led into the classroom. It was packed with children of all ages; the air was filled with the joyful noises children make at play. To the east of the school, on the other side of a fence, sat a row of houses referred to as "crack houses." They were small one-story units with no garages, sporting scraped edges of paint and the ungroomed yards. Cars lined the street. I looked over there warily, hoping it was a calm day in the neighborhood. We had been forewarned about the dangers of our environment.

None of the warnings were typical to my previous experiences. The staff had learned in our opening meetings that we regularly practiced three drills: the fire drill, the earthquake drill, and a third one that I had never faced before, the gunshot drill. Students were to lie flat on the floor so that any stray bullets coming through windows would not hit a child. They kept coats nearby to shield them from shards of shattering glass. The commands came quickly; the more we practiced, the faster the children would respond. Timing was crucial and instant obedience a necessity. It was often a dangerous area, I was told. We should be cautious about leaving the grounds and entering and exiting the parking lot. Gangs operated in the neighborhood and we were to be on the alert at all times to that possibility.

When the bell rang, I moved toward the line that I knew was my class. I use the word "line" loosely, because although the children were supposed to be in a semblance of order, they were stretched across everyone's space. I found this unusual for fifth graders, who should have been used to standing directly behind each other and quietly waiting. This group, however, was anything but silent. They were talking loudly, shoving each other, standing in twos and threes, and seemingly unaware of my presence. Finally I got their attention, even though the bell had not. Somehow we marched into the classroom I had tried so hard to make inviting.

The room itself was cold, dark, and small, and despite my efforts to cheer it up, it seemed dreary to me. The old Venetian blinds on the windows didn't reveal much light. The walls were gray. The chalkboard, though green, was faded. I had written *Welcome to Class* in the middle with yellow chalk. The floor was tiled, aged and scuffed. My desk took up one corner of the front area and bookcases lined the wall perpendicular to mine. The back area had a closet for more storage shelves. There was a lone bulletin board that I had covered with colorful paper and a fall design that brightened the front of the room. I was glad for that one cheery spot. Fresh flowers were on my desk; I hoped the children noticed the care and planning that had preceded their entry.

I had put the children's desks in rows to begin the year, thinking I would move them into groups of two and then maybe four, occasionally, as they learned to work on projects together. On the wall under the windows was a lone computer on a scarred table. It was well used and not the newest machine. Still, I was grateful to have even that, and had already set up a schedule for making sure children had computer time. I knew that many of the students would want a special time there.

In walked twenty-four totally unfamiliar faces. I admit that my nerves were pretty frayed by the time we got through the door. Mentally I added one more item to the day: practicing what a line should look like. I invited the children to find their own places and there were murmurs and restlessness as they clamored for a favorite spot—something I wasn't used to at all. Finally seated, they became quiet as I stood and waited.

Usually on the first day, the children are very well behaved, listening and giving the teacher a bit of a "honeymoon" period. I was uncertain whether my class would follow this pattern today. I smiled at my new students as we went over rules—I was using a soft voice, so they strained a bit to hear. I knew these moments would establish our relationship. The sea of faces began to seem dear to me. I put names to them throughout the morning, seeking to learn each one quickly and accurately.

One of the most important principles of education is how important initial learning is: what you learn first in any new situation stays with you.[5] I really wanted to get it

---

5   Hunter, Madeline. <u>Mastery Teaching</u>. El Segundo, CA: TIP

right on this important first day of school. The relationship between my class and me depended on my careful set-up of the rules and the year. This was not going to be easy. The children didn't trust me yet. Often trust came with the title of teacher, but I expected it to be harder for me here. I had planned to do what was "normal" for fifth graders, but I didn't know what normal was for my new students. They wanted to hear about me, and I wanted to know what they felt was important.

I soon realized that they had short attention spans and I wanted to keep that attention focused on useful and important skills for the day, so I adjusted the schedule to suit their needs. We took short breaks as needed as I introduced each new activity. We practiced the drills I mentioned before. Earthquake meant under the desk and gunshot on the floor. I had my stopwatch ready and we practiced until they had reduced their time to an acceptable amount. The children seemed to enjoy these exercises, plus the movement gave them a respite from the sitting and listening we had done in the beginning.

All was going well until it was time to go to the rest room. Since we had no bathroom in the classroom, we needed to march over to the main building; since classes were in session, we needed to cross the playground quietly. That was an impossible task. They were noisy, even as I took the time to practice walking in line. I had assumed that the five teachers they had had before me had taught them that same skill, but if that were true, those teachers had failed miserably—as did I in this endeavor. I quickly realized we wouldn't accomplish that elementary skill unless I could convince them of its importance.

I had no mentor on the staff, no one to explain to me

Publication. 1982, 1986, 1994 and 1996.

that these children were volatile when left to their own resources, and I had to be constantly vigilant about turning my back or allowing my new students the freedoms I usually had given my fifth graders. The girls seemed to do all right being sent into the bathroom two at a time. It was a disaster with the boys. Two were too many, I discovered, because I heard shouts and shoving—a situation I couldn't remedy without entering the boy's bathroom (which I would never do). I quickly adjusted and sent them in one by one.

What an amazing waste of time! I decided I would have to usurp a little of their recess time if they didn't speed up the process. Having mentors for new staff was an idea I was going to share with Miss Lanikin as soon as I could.

I had changed schools often, both due to moving to accommodate my husband's career and because of taking time off to raise my children. Consequently, I knew that in any new situation, you had to prove yourself to the students, the staff, the principal, the parents, and even to the janitor. No one here knew yet that I was caring, highly motivated, and so willing to go the distance for my children. Everyone was waiting and watching, and I hoped I could succeed.

I was amazed at some of the differences I found; I soon began keeping a mental list of things that happened in this school that had never happened in my classroom before. Pasting projects seemed to totally entice my students. To my shock, though, they weren't interested in being creative. Rather, some of them smeared their hands with the paste, let it dry and peeled it off! They merely used the supplies to form a diversion for themselves. Of course, I knew the children were also testing the limits, so it was easy to remedy the paste problem. I took the bottles away, telling them it was their choice if they wanted it back, because there was to be no wasting of it in our classroom.

Once they turned their attention to it, they did engage

in the project I chose; I asked them to make a collage all about themselves, for me to learn more about their wants, needs, and desires. Many of them had to wait to finish their project because of the glue situation, but I knew that I had made progress with many of these very special students. They began to accept that I had control over the classroom, and that letting me be in charge would ultimately make them comfortable. By noon I knew all of their names.

At lunchtime, I entered the teachers' room to eat. Mary Chapman was sitting there looking despondent, so I inquired how her morning had gone. She said she had handed out math papers and one third-grade boy said, "I don't want to do this shit!" We laughed and the tension began to ease a bit. Mrs. Chapman had been on the staff for three years. She was a stereotype of a teacher—clipboard in hand, always prepared, and eager to achieve her goals. However, being good students ourselves doesn't always prepare us for the children who don't care about learning and working.

I looked around to observe who else I could get acquainted with in my few short minutes. The only people there were white.

"Where is everyone?" I asked.

I was told that the black aides and teachers ate in a classroom most of the time.

"Why?"

"They gather in Mrs. Jelop's room," shrugged Mrs. Chapman.

"I would love to get to know them better," I replied.

Were the color lines inescapable? I didn't want that to happen! Surely we could treat each other as fellow staff members and enjoy each other's company. I wanted to eat with and get acquainted with everyone. I didn't have time to pursue that problem at the moment, as my stomach churned and my nerves began to dictate where my thoughts should be—on how to survive the rest of the day.

Math class began our afternoon, and it was fun. I discovered that my stopwatch was fascinating to my class. They loved the time tests I had laid out on shelves for them to pick up themselves. Each student could advance once he or she got 100% on each step within the five-minute time period I gave them. This is an old-fashioned idea that is so useful in memorizing multiplication tables. It's hard work for the teacher, because the tests have to be corrected each day, but it is well worth the effort.

I taught my class a new process: instead of me handing out the tests directly to them, they would need to get up, get the paper, and return to their seats in an orderly manner. They, of course, were at different levels, which were determined by the tests. I had silent signals I would use to cue them for each step. Additionally, I would count down from ten and they needed to be seated by the time I reached "one." They seemed to enjoy the challenge, and liked using this system of quiet signals. I knew that I would have to re-teach the system each day the first week.

"Can we do those time tests tomorrow?" they asked. "They were fun!"

"We surely will," I replied, smiling my agreement to the eager faces.

Recess was another learning experience for me, as we made our way to the playground. There were courts for playing basketball, but very little else for them to occupy their time. I mentally noted how we'd have to learn some games to help them stay out of trouble during their fifteen minutes of free time.

At the end of the day, I went back over to the office and discovered that one wing of the school had spent the entire afternoon on the ground in a gunshot drill, as the police had apprehended a felon and had guns drawn right by the north windows of the school. The children stayed flat on the floor until the police left the area. I certainly knew at that point that this would not be the kind of year I was used to having. Usually my only worry was to make sure my children were learning at the pace they needed and receiving the best instruction I could possibly give. There was so much more to be concerned about here, for the sake of the children and the community.

Chapter Four

The Students: My Primary Focus

Steadman towered over everyone—even me! —and was restless. I could tell from the beginning that he was smart and alert, but I was told he got in trouble all of the time. I didn't want that to continue; I yearned for him to understand that I was here to help him, to meet his needs and try my best to prepare him (and every child) for the world ahead of them.

"Isn't that just a form of stereotyping?" Steadman asked me, as he commented on a character in one of our stories. *Wow*, I thought, as I looked at this bright, eager boy. That was certainly not a common analysis from most fifth graders I had taught.

I smile a lot as I teach. I think body language and facial expressions can influence how a child feels in any given situation. I tried to project strong, happy feelings for my students as they got to know me. Steadman's mind was very bright and he processed everything quickly, but I really didn't know what his world was like; I could only hope I was making a difference.

Mia turned around to talk, constantly looking at me to

see if I would do anything to stop what she knew was wrong. I moved toward her desk and stood with my hand on her books—it was enough to alert to her my meaning. She was bright and eager and so much fun. I was careful to observe what helped her to concentrate on the task at hand, and I tried my best to communicate my desire for her to succeed. She was willing to work hard, but the boys around her were a distraction, as she was ten going on twenty-one. How I yearned to re-capture her childhood for her. "I like your gold buttons," she said on that first day of school—such a good combination of shyness and boldness.

At the beginning of each year, I wanted to contact parents by phone or in person.[6] It was a time for me to bond with them as well as with the children, so I called and tried to bridge the gap between school and home. Could the parents in this school bond with me to give the maximum help toward the success of their child? I hoped so. I tried to communicate the fact that if they were my partners, and if they praised what was happening at school, the children would improve more rapidly.

"What did my kid do?" was the usual response to my phone call, when I first identified myself.

"LaMar has had a great start to his year!" I replied. Or, "Ebony is doing a wonderful job with her reading." I gave honest praise whenever I could. At the very least, I quickly reassured each parent: "Your child is not in trouble at all." These calls were meant to be positive, so the parents could hear what good things their children were accomplishing. The fact that the parents heard a friendly voice helped them view the school in a favorable light.

I hoped that fact would hold true here. I wanted the

---

6   "Inner City Schooling." University of Michigan. http://sitemaker.umich.edu?mitchellyellin.356/parental-involvement.

parents to come to me with any doubts they had instead of making negative comments about the school. "If you have any concerns or questions, please feel free to call me," I always told them. I knew that if they were upset about something and commented about it directly to their children, it would affect the children's ability to do their best.

I wanted to talk to all parents in the first two weeks of school. This gave me a chance to say mainly positive, encouraging things about their child. It also gave me an opportunity to meet the parents via phone and have a little familiarity with their voices and their attitudes before parent-teacher conferences came at the end of the first quarter. It was difficult to reach everyone: some of my students had no phones, while others answered with reluctance. However, most of the parents I contacted were fun to visit with and easy to engage in conversation. I was feeling all right about my progress in that area. However, I had twenty-four students and I could only make about three or four calls a night before I fell into bed, exhausted.

Sometimes, if I couldn't reach them by phone, I tried to go to the parents' home—something that I was told could be dangerous. Nevertheless, I forged ahead after school the second week. Mikayle lived just behind the school, so I thought I could just walk there quickly and talk with her parents, despite the warning I had been given about doing so. When I approached her house, I noticed that black plastic covered all of the windows. I gently knocked and several small children opened the door. They were bright-eyed and welcoming, but quickly returned to their play.

I stepped into a room with no furniture. Mikayle was a very tiny little girl whom all the children teased, and I didn't know why. I wanted to stop that as fast as I could. She never completed her homework and rarely talked in class, never volunteering an answer. I was concerned and wanted to figure out why she was struggling.

I ventured into the next room, which might have been a dining room, but again the only furnishing was a mattress on the floor, with an older lady—her grandmother, I learned—on the mattress. There must have been eight children running around in the house, all of them ten years old or younger.

I knelt as the old woman said, "I just don't feel well today." I empathized with her, trying to no avail to find out where the parents were. I learned that Mikayle ran the streets on her own a lot and was "wild" and hard to control. This was not the case in the classroom. She was shy and avoided the other children, who teased her mercilessly any time they were out of earshot. (I was told this by one of the other students who seemed to feel sorry for Mikayle.) I told the grandmother that the girl missed a lot of school and fell behind so quickly.

"Does Mikayle bring home her schoolwork for you to see?" I asked.

"No," she replied.

"I'm hoping she will do her homework," I commented, though I didn't want to prolong a conversation the older woman didn't feel well enough to handle.

I looked around at the other children in the house. *Who are they?* I thought.

"Are these all your grandchildren? I asked. She nodded her head.

"Do the parents live here as well?" I inquired.

She sighed, "No," and her eyes began to close.

"I would like to help Mikayle do her work," I said. "Can she stay after school for my help?" The elderly lady smiled and nodded, but I knew she needed to rest, and was only appeasing me. I assured her I would write a note to her the day before Mikayle was to stay after school for help with me, and I hurried out of the small house.

How was Mikayle going to complete fifth grade, let alone middle school and high school, when she had no support system for learning and the other children in the class seemed to ridicule her at every opportunity? I was disheartened by worry. This was an amazing challenge and would be a top priority for me. I didn't want this small, timid child to be abused by the others—something that I began to control by going outside during every recess.

One of the boys in the class was little Tyrell. He was small but mighty, and so smart. He worked hard and loved the computer—never wanted to get off of it. I soon learned that the best preventative for him was loss of computer time. Each student had an allotted time to work on our one computer. If they didn't stop when their time was up, they lost the privilege the next time. Tyrell guarded his time well. He was quick at learning and I praised his abilities to his mother. She was a single mom who worked all of the time. She didn't trust me and didn't respond to my calls. It would take a long time for her to understand that my motives were pure love for the children in my class and an all-consuming desire to have them achieve the best they could in the short time that we called fifth grade.

LaMar fell asleep in class every afternoon as I read to them after lunch. That actually happened to a lot of children. I soon learned that most of them stayed up until eleven o'clock, sometimes-past midnight. I had never heard of that! I had a lot to learn.

LaMar closed down in the afternoon, just sat there and wouldn't work—couldn't work. His home was a noisy place with several families living together. His father was in jail and all was not well at home for them. How does a child succeed and learn without sleep, support, and structure? [7] I didn't know the answer, but I knew that at many times in the year I found myself saying, "There is too much to fix!" But where was I to begin? Which problem, when solved, would help the most?

Ebony had attention-deficit hyperactivity disorder, or ADHD. Every day she was to take her medicine, or I would have to "scrape her off the ceiling." There was no level of concentration available to her. Her eyes darted every which way—her hands fidgeted and she couldn't begin to focus on her work. She hated to take the medicine, but I saw no way for her to advance without it. Her grandmother was raising her, as her mother worked full-time and her father had left many years before that. Her grandmother was sweet and compassionate. She wanted to do everything she could for Ebony. I called her many times to foster support and bridge the gap between home and school.

Deasia came to school one day in tears. Her mother had kicked her out of the house. She just got mad at her and told her never to come back. She went to her grandma's, a better place it seemed ... but that was my opinion, not Deasia's. She longed for her mother to want her and come and get her. She tried to work, but how does one concentrate when one's life has been turned upside down? What egregious error had she made to deserve this? I only heard Deasia's side, of course, but I wondered about how little it took to end this mother-daughter relationship.

Mary was the only white girl in the class. She came a little later in the school year and was eager to please in her new environment. I learned how strange this setting was

7   Cairney, Trevor. The 4th "R" Rest! "Literacy, Families and Learning,"http://trevorcairney.blogspot.com/2009/03/4th-r-rest.html.3/11/2009

for her when she came into school late one morning, and I asked her why.

"My mom sent me to the store to buy a bottle of milk. It was a glass bottle and a black man walked by me, bumped me, and it broke all over the ground and got all over me." She was late because she had to go home and change. Being a stranger and a different race within a closed setting was difficult for anyone, much less a child. Seeing her struggle contributed to my desire to create racial balance here, though I knew there was no easy solution to bullies in any culture.

Reidel sat at the back of the room and never looked at me when I smiled at him. He rarely came to school. All of his brothers were gang members. I yearned to be able to reach him in some way; he behaved and listened, but rarely completed an assignment. I tried to sit beside him and help but that made him uncomfortable. He was in his own world, and often it didn't include school. I was an oddity to him—someone who didn't fit his picture of an adult or a teacher. His world was volatile and unruly and I was an anomaly in that world. He looked at me with distrust. How I wished I could have bridged the gap between home and school for him, but I could never talk to his parents, nor did they attend conferences. They had no phone and I wasn't allowed to go to their property. He was only in the classroom the equivalent of two months, finally dropping out without a word of explanation.

Ada needed attention. She was very overweight, which precipitated a lot of teasing from her peers. She was outspoken and hostile at first, and I knew she was hurting for attention and a good friend. Over the years I had learned that every child needs a friend to whom he or she can relate and tell his or her stories, problems, and wishes. I watched Ada carefully, knowing that I might need to intervene and be a sounding board. I was hoping I could gain her trust.

My husband was so totally supportive and understanding about the hours I was putting into this new assignment. He looked at me one night, however, and said that it would be better if I didn't work such long hard hours. "Things will work out," he said. With those kind words I hoped he was right, and fell asleep only to awaken in the middle of the night. Thoughts immediately began to crowd out sleep, as they so often could do to me. I tried flipping my pillow to the cold side in an attempt to get a fresh start on relaxing. Losing sleep in this way became a weekly problem.

Chapter Five

Adjusting

One day, I arrived at school at 6:30 a.m. The janitor by this time knew my schedule and was in the parking lot to meet me. He said, "There is a homeless guy sleeping by the front door, so come in the back way with me." He went on to say that he would wake the man up and get him out of there before the children started to arrive. As I walked toward the back of the building, I glanced at the sleeping man. He was white, with a hat perched on his head, and he was inside a well-used sleeping bag. His face was wrinkled, making it hard to discern his age—it was impossible to know what circumstances brought him to the point of needing to sleep outside in front of the school. He was under the overhang that covered the front entryway. Though he looked peaceful in his sleep, a flash of remorse went through my mind. I thought that could have been my father, if a family who cared for him didn't surround him.

My mind quickly shifted to the problems I was facing before school began.

Usually, I tried to make copies before the other teachers arrived, because there was only one Xerox machine. We waited in line to get anything done. Today the paper stuck together and too many sheets were running through. Nothing was working out as planned. I bagged that assignment and decided on another math lesson. My experience helped me shift quickly into another lesson plan. I stood at the front door watching the children play and thinking about the day before.

How would I adjust to the needs of children in this culture and economic situation? Their world was so different from mine, and I yearned to find the right approach to learning for children. I went home to a quiet atmosphere, whereas they went home to noise, confusion, and a very crowded environment. Most children were not as happy about the assignments as I was: homework was easy for me to set up for them, but did they even have an opportunity to sit in a quiet place to do the work? My telephone calls always had noise in the background. I knew from talking to the children that many of the homes had more than one family living there. On a sunny day, as I drove through the neighborhood, many people were outside, and the music from their boom boxes could be heard from a distance.

My philosophy about instructions came from years of college, years of experience, and easily fifty workshops that I either taught or attended in order to learn about current and better teaching approaches. I was passionate about doing the best for my students. They became my own children, so to speak, and I worked non-stop to do all in my power to help them succeed. I am happy that I can say that these same feelings have been present in so many teachers that I have met and worked with over many years. As a body of workers we are certainly in the profession because of our hearts that are sincerely open to helping children. I have great pride in the fact that we believe strongly in helping enhance the lives of the children.

I have come to believe that children shouldn't be grouped by ability permanently. My teaching skills evolved to where I taught to the fastest learner, so they wouldn't be bored, and I formed small skill groups to keep reviewing until all children learned the concepts we were working on. The skill groups changed to adapt to each new study set. I often put children in heterogeneous groups having many skill levels so they could help each other. I didn't want any of them to think they were labeled as slow learners; their self-esteem was fragile, and that would never help them. After the first couple of weeks, I tried to put children in groups by putting their desks together. Big mistake! The noise level went way up and the work level went down.

At the end of the day I sat in Jerome's office, feeling forlorn. The head teacher listened compassionately as I explained what happened when I tried to group the children to work together. He said, "These kids, despite the fact that they know each other pretty well, don't trust each other much, and they don't want anyone in the class to find out that they might not know something being taught or how to do what was being asked of them. They basically lack self-confidence," he concluded.

His message to me was that they were much more comfortable with the desks arranged in rows. "They've never worked in groups before and have no experience of cooperation, as they have been in rows all through school," he added.

I was amazed. "So you're saying that now, when adolescence is setting in, it will probably not work to their benefit—and certainly not to mine—to try to teach them in groups?" He nodded.

I thanked him so much for that insight, yet I hoped I'd somehow be able to achieve a keener sense of cooperation between now and the end of my year. A classroom needed to become a caring community. Whew! This was an immense challenge, and I was starting from ground zero.

I know from the experiences I have had in today's schools—a few years after I retired—that most small children are put at tables facing each other all the time. I believe that sometimes children need to face the front of the class and be by themselves. That's why I do believe in rows at certain times and cooperation, pairing, and teams at other times. I think all of us need some time to be alone to think by ourselves. This takes into consideration the introverts in the classroom who really need alone time, and it gives equal voice to those children who are overly social who would work better on their own at times, because they easily fall into the trap of visiting with the children whom they are facing. I went right back to my room and re-arranged the seating to rows. I could see the relief on the faces of the children as they entered the schoolroom the next morning. Peace and quiet settled in, and I learned a good lesson that seemed to please the children.

My class as a whole was smart! They learned quickly. For example, during the first days of school I wanted them to memorize a poem so they could point to something new and tangible that they had learned. I had the poem written on the board as they walked into class in the morning. We said it in unison, and the second time through I erased one word in each row. We said it in unison again. Pretty soon I erased two more words, then three, and so on, as they easily inserted the correct response. They loved it; to a student, they knew that poem all through the year, and many more poems, as I saw their enthusiasm for learning this way.

Certainly not every day was an easy experience. It was impossible to plan a full week's work in advance; I analyzed each day, as most teachers do, and knew that I either had to review, switch gears, or forge ahead, and it was not always according to those weekly lesson plans that we were required to turn into the principal.

As I stood at the door, that morning after the copy machine wouldn't work and I had bagged my math lesson, I decided to try the rap music and rhythm tapes that I got to show a new way for them to learn. When the bell rang, I rounded up my group and we marched into place. When the room quieted down I turned on the tape and let them listen for a few minutes. Soon they were tapping their feet and clapping to the beat.

"O.K.," I said. "Let's do the multiplication tables with this." We formed some noisy groups and they actually worked together! Each group performed; I was amazed at the talent they showed off. Could we learn math facts more quickly using music? I thought I would continue to use those rap tapes off and on in almost every subject. It felt pretty good to see them having controlled fun.

Next we worked on time tests, which they were learning to like after some initial groans. They learned the multiplication tables quickly and loved to show off by passing tests. I had the different levels of tests in trays on one side of the room. They all knew which one they were on and where to go to pick up the one for the day.

"Get your time tests," I said, and each student got up. I turned my back to the chaos to grab my stopwatch. When I turned around, in walked the principal and head teacher. *Oh great*, I thought. I knew that this was organized chaos, but the administrators had no idea that there was a method to the madness. I smiled and I began to count. This was a signal for my students to return to their desks; luckily, they all did just that. The principal smiled, much to my relief, and I began the test: "On your mark, get set, go!" They were off and writing as fast as they could.

Over the years I have used various symbols to give the

children as a signal for their immediate silence. I've used rain sticks, music boxes, clapping, hand signals; anything can work if the students are trained at the beginning and practice them, so that the silence is instant and fun for them. It doesn't get boring when they are changed monthly.

After the time tests, Ms. Lanikin lectured the students about behavior. I could see their faces go blank and knew they had turned her off the minute she said things like *you must* and *you can't* and *don't do* this and that. "I will take your recess away if there are any more fights out there!" she announced. I hoped the children would heed her words, but prior experience taught me that lectures don't do much good, especially if the children turned off their hearing. Threats become a challenge to them ... a challenge to test the limits!

I really didn't want Ms. Lanikin to take away their recess. I knew that fights and skirmishes occurred at recess time at an alarming rate—something she had known would happen from past experiences—and she was seeking ways to curb deviant behavior. This was a new experience for me; even a single fight happening in the previous schools I had taught in was extremely rare. Still, I knew that our world was getting more volatile, especially with the gangs located in this very neighborhood. That, in addition to constant violence in the media, created a breeding ground for just what was happening.

I first began teaching in a small rural town in Montana. The children came from two-parent farm homes for the most part, and they walked into the classroom, sat down, and folded their hands on top of their desks. If there was a fight, it was mild and easily solved. In this inner city, by contrast, children often began a fight with fists, and then went home and came back with a knife or gun. Ms. Lanikin felt the weight of her responsibility and I sympathized with what she was saying.

I went home that night feeling all right about the day. My only problem was that because we worked so hard on time tests, and many other activities during the day, I still had a huge mound of papers to correct. Everything was looked at and graded, put into neat piles, and packed in my brief case. When at last it was time to sleep, that state eluded me again, and my mind began to work through what had happened when the principal came into the room. I began to think about the playground and what I knew about dealing with it.

One of the many workshops I had attended was called, "Dealing with Difficult Children." The main thrust of this (and similar) workshops was to demonstrate the fact that children need to have power to control their own situation. The children in the inner city seemed to rebel against authoritarian methods. They didn't want to be told what to do. I found it far easier to give them choices—but they were all *my* choices, so I was in control. Giving them the power to choose helped them through some touchy situations. Everyone needs to feel powerful, and with my students this was particularly true.

For example, if a student didn't complete an assignment, I would say, "You can finish this work now, while we are having a break, or at recess time. Which would you like to do?" If they said they didn't want to complete it, I would say, "That is not one of your choices." I would then repeat the previous choices I gave them. It was a broken record approach, but it worked. The student would get the assignment done.

The playground provided another example of techniques that were needed in the inner city that I had not used in my prior experience. I was astounded at how quickly tempers flared and physical fights began. I am a fairly small woman, and my students were commonly about my size or definitely bigger. To stop the fights quickly, I was taught to go behind the aggressor and put my arms around that child to pull him or her away. It happened often. Even as they came in from play and stood in line to get drinks, my students might start punching each other—especially if I wasn't standing right beside them. I learned never to leave them alone at the drinking fountain. I had to find a way to help them learn the self-control they needed to succeed in school and ultimately in their lives. I knew I had to put a plan in place early in the year.

I decided to make class meetings the first step in teaching my pupils that differences of opinion can be worked out in better ways than fighting. I had a notebook at the door as they walked in after recess. They were to put their names in it if they wanted to speak at our next class meeting, which was arranged for a specific time during the week. At the class meeting time, they were able to express what went wrong or what other student had made them upset, and then we had a sort of mini-trial.

All people named told their side of the story and the class decided who should have a consequence for their behavior. The children gave suggestions for the consequence and the guilty child got to choose his or her consequence. A consequence was defined as some action that would help the child to be able to not do the act or offense again. A consequence had to contain the three *R*'s of the class meeting: it had to be *related* to what had happened, *respectful* of the person who had made the mistake, and *reasonable* for the child and for the offense.

The children took some time to be good at finding consequences. They often showed favoritism to their friends, and friendships often followed color lines. If a white student or a Hispanic student was the offender, the other 95% of the children who were black could easily bond against the minority child. Seeing this happen only contributed to my desire for children to be integrated with a healthy mix of races, so that no race was dominant. It was a harsh neighborhood for minority children. This would be true in an all-white or all-Hispanic school as well; no race should dominate another, in my opinion.

Our first class meeting began that process. The culprit was a white boy who didn't follow a rule in kickball. The students suggested that he never get to play kickball again. Patiently I asked, "Is that respectful toward Jim? Is that reasonable that he should never play again? Is the consequence related to what happened in the game?" They agreed that the consequence was related to the game, but reluctantly they began to understand that it wasn't very reasonable, nor was it respectful. I smiled inwardly; this would be slow going but I wouldn't give up, because working out problems was what I was trying to teach. I wanted to tell Ms. Lanikin about this process, so I asked for a conference with her after school the next day. I mulled over how I would present my ideas, knowing that she might not agree.

Tyrone presented an example I think about often. He had a physical handicap and was born with a deformed leg. He lived with a stepfather and his mother, and things weren't easy for him. He chose to find a way to fight with any new student that entered my room. He would beat them up when my back was turned on the playground or in the restroom. After the second time that this happened, I was walking him over to the office and I asked him how he was feeling now, knowing he had to appear before the principal. His reply always makes me sad, when I think about it. He said, "I wish I hadn't done it, Mrs. Hilton." I was trying so hard to teach these children ways to cope, but was it ever going to be enough? Here were children who were smart and eager, with quick tempers and impossible problems often causing them to get in trouble.

I went to the principal's office after school. She had made good the threat of cutting off recess as a response to misbehavior. I talked with her a long time, explaining how much I wanted my class to get better at solving social problems. I explained about the class meetings I was trying to have, and asked if she would allow us to go out by ourselves if I always took them out and supervised. She promised she would think about it. I left the office feeling sad and lonely.

The next morning, just as I was getting ready to leave for school at about 5:45, the phone rang. It was Tyrone's mother, Eva, whom I had talked to quite a bit, trying to work things out with her to help Tyrone feel better about school and the other children. She was such a hard-working lady; she worked at a local nursing home and put in very long hours. Her story was a sad one.

"My husband beat me up last night," she said.

"I'm so sorry," I replied. "How can I help?"

"He left, so I took the kids, grabbed all the food I could get before he came back, and left the house."

"Where are you now?" I asked.

"I went to the homeless shelter downtown; it's the best one, but I had to bring food. I put it in the refrigerator, and when I got up this morning, someone had taken it!"

"I need the directions to where you are, and I'll bring what I can!" I said. "I'll be there in about thirty minutes."

"I'll watch for you," she replied and hung up the phone.

As quickly as I could, I packed a box of supplies for her and decided cash was important as well. Finding my way into the inner city wasn't easy for me, but luckily she had given me good directions and as promised was standing at the edge of the curb when I arrived.

I had her get into the front seat of the car. "Thank you so much," she said, with tears in her eyes that matched mine, as I handed her the items I brought. She left quickly so as to not leave her two boys alone in the shelter.

On the way back to school, I thought to myself, *I would have been upset at Tyrone for not doing his homework, if I didn't know those circumstances.*

So much was setting my students up for failure. Tears flowed easily for me those days, and I so wished I knew how to guarantee that the lives of these children would have a chance to succeed. I went back to school wondering what I could do to help this family.

Tyrone came to school and surprisingly settled right into his work. I didn't mention what had happened, nor did he say anything about it. I knew he was not going home that night, that he was headed back to the shelter. I was unsure how I could assist him. He was too proud to ask for help. Did he need to talk to someone? Was he feeling frightened and alone? Had this happened before to his family? Would it happen again? Should I say something to him, or would he prefer not to talk about it?

"Are you and your brother walking today?" I asked. He nodded his head. "You have a longer walk, "I ventured to say, probing a bit to show I would help if needed.

"It's not too far," he said. "We'll be all right," I knew from his reticence that he didn't want to talk about it. Soon they were back in their home. There wasn't another incident that I knew about during my time with them.

Chapter Six

Special Help

Our school had a Child Development specialist who seemed to me to take the place of a school counselor, but I was never sure what he did. I went to him after I watched Tyrone leave school on foot. Tyrone walked with a limp, due to his deformed foot, and I knew he would have a longer walk to the shelter. I wanted to help him, but I didn't know what the right approach was in this situation.

Driving around town was still not easy for me. I lost my way often and had problems with directions. Many times I called my husband in the middle of the city and asked him how to get where I was going (the GPS was not invented at that time). So I went to our Child Development person and told him the situation. I asked if there was help for this family or if he would take more food over to them, if I provided more monetary support.

"Oh, I never go to that neighborhood!" he said. "It's not safe."

I thought his answer was very strange for a person whose job was to help the children in this neighborhood. Of course he was a bit more immune to those situations than I was.

He added, "Tyrone's family always needed help and I can't continually bail them out."

His reaction surprised me, but it was another learning tool. Was I vulnerable to giving too much help, or was he calloused and unfeeling? I didn't want to judge this man without examining my own role in these situations. I am not prone to being critical of my co-workers. I admired the roles of each department and found their functions necessary and important.

Most of the special help at Rosa Parks was excellent; the department included a speech therapist and special reading people who worked tirelessly to help children. I loved working with them and sought their help whenever I could. All children were assessed and special needs were addressed. After-school programs helped many children through the year. It just seemed like there was so much to fix—lack of parental involvement, the struggle for each family just to get by. The school was a safe haven in many respects.

One important program was the free lunch. All children received free breakfast and lunch every day. The lunchroom was clean and well run. The cooks and aides did a great job of helping children get good nutrition.

As I walked into the lunchroom with my children straggling behind me, I noticed the calm atmosphere and quiet, well-behaved students at the tables. Bill, the P.E. teacher, was in charge here and he was impressive. My students looked at him with respect and did as he asked. He had a wonderful way with the students, but he had still not spoken to me. I smiled at him and he nodded at me. That was the first sign of his acknowledging my presence. He told my students where to sit and how to behave. I'm happy to report that I worked with Bill on a committee later in the year and he became friendlier. We shared our thoughts about curriculum and he seemed open to my ideas.

His unfriendliness toward me in retrospect seemed to be a waiting to see if I really cared about the children. I believe he knew I did by the end of the year.

My students had P.E. right after lunch, so that was an easy transition as the lunchroom turned into the gym and the fifth graders helped put up the tables and get themselves ready to participate.

As I walked into the teachers' lounge, I reflected on my day. I was already exhausted and the day was only half over. The faculty lunchroom was no cheerier than I was. No one was there. I looked up at the windows, which were small rectangles covered with gray drapes. The tables were rejects from classrooms, old and cracked. The refrigerator was ancient, small, and ugly.

I got out my lunch and wished I were anyplace else but here. A couple of others walked into the room, quickly sat down, and began to eat. I tried to strike up a conversation, but it seemed like no one felt up to anything but eating and getting back to work. I thought back to other schools in which teachers compared notes and ideas cheerily as they ate. Maybe there would be days like that, but today wasn't one of them. I was in a gray mood on a gray day in a gray room.

I straightened my shoulders and tried to talk myself into starting the second half of the day. My students would soon be back to the room and I needed to be there, greet them with a smile, and have some exciting activities ready. It would certainly take some effort for me. I got up and moved out the door, across the quiet playground, and into my trailer-classroom.

Chapter Seven

Reading

One subject close to my heart was reading. I loved to read, and I loved to read to the children. I expected the children to be inspired by my enthusiasm, but of course reality never equaled daydreams, even though the school was set up to promote reading.

The library was wonderfully equipped and lots of choice books were available. The school also held a Book Fair in the fall, hoping to put lots of books into the hands of the children. The librarian worked so hard to get it set up, and it lasted a full week. Many books were sold, a good number of them into the hands of my students. However, much to my dismay, the librarian reported that many of the checks bounced due to insufficient funds; moreover, when the fair got busy and she couldn't keep an eye on everyone, some books were stolen. She did not want to continue holding book fairs if these behaviors were standard. I knew that the parents in this community wanted their children to read, and the staff certainly did, so I was very sad that they wouldn't have this opportunity again for a while.

Luckily, we still had our library time each week to make

sure borrowed books remained available. I spent a lot of time teaching my class about the responsibility of returning the books they borrowed to the library. The reading time after lunch in my classroom was one of the student's favorite times. They loved the stories and got fully involved in the books I chose. Sometimes, however, they fell asleep. Lunch, a warm classroom, a quiet reading voice, and a likely lack of sleep the night before certainly set up the atmosphere for drowsiness. Most of the time, though, the children cherished the time after lunch when I read to them. Often they sighed when I started to close the book and asked me to keep reading. That always pleased me, because to get caught up in a story was the beginning of love of reading—a gift they would keep forever.

We were studying American History in fifth grade. What better book could I get for them to read than *Fighting Ground* by Avi? I was excited. This story told about the Revolution and the main character was a young boy, Jonathan. The story is only 157 pages and begins when the protagonist is working in the field with his dad. He hears the bell in the town square toll for any able person to come and fight in one of the smaller battles of the Revolutionary War. Jonathan dreamed of doing just that. He had a glorified idea of what fighting was all about, as do so many young people in our world.

Jonathan decided to take his father's musket and join the small troop determined to fight the Hessian army. This was a band of men helping the British quash the rebels, our forefathers. The story takes place within a period of twenty-four hours. The point of the story is subtle and difficult for fifth graders to comprehend; I wondered if any of my smart readers would discover the real point of Avi's book. In the story, Jonathan is captured and taken care of by his captors. At one point he asks the question, "Who is my enemy?"

The people with whom he fought didn't protect him, but his enemies did. What is the point of war? Why do we kill innocent, kind, empathetic people? Who has the right to kill anyone?

I knew that as we read, many children less able to comprehend would find this book difficult. We read it over a two-week period and my students' discussions were often interesting. Some circled the meaning, while others just thought the fighting was exciting.

All of a sudden Steadman raised his hand.

"I get it!!" he said. "Our enemies can sometimes be our friends. They are people just like we are. It is all in our point of view."

My heart jumped with excitement.

"Wow!" I said. "How many of you agree with Steadman?"

Hands began to go up, and I was overjoyed. This story began to make my students think. Suddenly the American Revolution was going to mean more than a date and time long ago. History was stepping into their world and making them connect with it, making them have a point of view.

Today was a good day, I thought, as I cleaned my desk after school. Despite the noise and the horns honking from the street beside my room, I was feeling pretty good. I looked at my watch and realized it was really getting late. I didn't like it to be completely dark outside before I left. I grabbed the papers I needed to correct and my purse, and started for the door.

As I stepped out on the classroom stoop, I suddenly stopped. The loud noises were coming from the basketball courts in front of me that were crowded with older boys— really, young men. It was almost totally dark, with only the streetlight to give the players a view of the ball court. Suddenly my heart started beating faster. I was frightened by what I saw. I was alone, and it was dark, but the real fear was that I didn't know the people on the playground, and they were a different race. The court was chaotic with rowdy players shouting at each other, and I couldn't tell whether it was playful banter or anger. My thoughts quickly shifted to articles about gangs circling a lone person; the palms of my hands began to sweat, and my breathing grew short and labored.

How could I cross the playground and get to my car? In actuality, when I looked around, it appeared that no one was paying any attention to me. All the men were African-American, and I berated myself by wondering if I would feel this fear if they had all been white. I knew that not any one race was immune from harassing women. I shook my head, wondering if it was normal to feel fear about different races, or if I would have felt the same if the court had been filled with white men, or a mixture of both races. I didn't know the answer to that, but I summoned my courage and started to walk across the edge of the basketball court. No one even noticed me, this middle-aged white woman, and I safely entered the main building and went out the front door.

Jerry Large, in an article in the *Seattle Times*, recently wrote about this very issue: "Tests show 75% of white people and half of black people unconsciously associate black people with negative traits and white people with positive traits." (He suggests taking one of the tests yourself, available at http://implicit.harvard.edu.[8]) I felt terrible about my reaction. I knew positive experiences could erase negative thoughts, and I wanted to have lots of experience to erase those inevitable attitudes. I wanted to be in the 25% that didn't see a difference.

---

8   Large, Jerry. "Unconscious Bias is Real Challenge." The Seattle Times. July 9, 2010.

Let's blur those color lines, I thought to myself. *There is no need for them*. Experiences help change lives, and I was hoping I could get comfortable in my new environment. I felt color lines in the school when people of like race stayed away from the lunchroom to eat together, but I didn't feel it in any way with my students. I did feel a sort of distrust aimed at me at times when I talked with parents who didn't know me and were unsure of my motives in calling them. Could they learn to know and trust me? Were the color lines always going to be there? I hoped not.

Chapter Eight

Conferences

It was teacher conference time. I slaved over the grades, averaging all those percentage points. It wasn't yet time to hand out report cards, but I wanted to have a sure idea about where each student's grades stood.

LaMar kept falling asleep in class and wasn't doing his work, and I reflected on his sparse row of grades. How could I again communicate to his mother that he needed more rest and support to succeed? I had talked to her in the first weeks of school, but lately I hadn't seen much change in LaMar, nor had I talked to his mother.

Later that afternoon I was called to the phone. It was a court advocate for LaMar. Apparently one or both of his parents were accused of a crime. The advocate, though kind, could not discuss the case with me and just needed me to be aware of LaMar's situation. She also asked how his schoolwork was going. I communicated my concern in hopes she might be able to give him a bit of support toward his homework. I knew under the circumstances that LaMar's parents wouldn't attend a conference. She was my liaison to the home.

As I returned to my room, I just felt sad. Life here was

not all about succeeding in school, or doing homework. It was about surviving. Perhaps my conferences would be a new experience in discovering how to help the parents at the same time as understanding their situation. Again I lamented, "There is too much to fix. Where do we begin in the lives of people that feel trapped into a survival mode on low income and in hard situations?"

My head was beginning to hurt, but mostly I was feeling sad for LaMar. He couldn't catch up very easily without the tools of sleep and a peaceful environment to succeed. I truly wanted to do what was best for this student, but he was so quiet and unmotivated. Now I began to understand why. I also knew that as he matured, even in a poor situation, he needed to take charge of himself. My own personal experiences about life played into my feeling about this.

I wanted to instill in LaMar the feelings I had about survival, but he was too young and hurting too much to take hold and begin to study. His capabilities were so tied up in his life situation, as was true of many of the children. His past skills were not a solid enough foundation for him to build upon. His grade school years were filled with absences and neglect. There were too many holes to fill. His parent's lives were not child-centered because they were just coping with their ability to survive.

Many of the parents were young, and there were a lot of alcohol- and drug-related problems in their homes. This puts a barrier up to solving problems for their children when they have so many of their own. "In communities of all sizes and shapes, parents face multiple challenges that may inhibit their ability to raise and support their children. The U.S. adolescent birth rate is now 43 for every 1000 families in the 15-19 year old age group."[9] Many of these young women

---

9   "Healthy Families and Children." Solutions for America www.

don't have the skills to raise their children. My mother kept my family together with a maturity that matched her years, as she was in her late thirties when I was born.

Mikayle's grades had improved for a while, because of my attention and work after school with her. Her home situation, however, had not improved. I talked to some of the students who so often just dismissed her as being hopeless. I wondered if her grandma would be well enough to come to the conference.

Conferences began at 4:00 p.m. after school and continued until 8:00 the first evening. One of the first parents to arrive was Steadman's mother. She was a large lady, very powerful looking, and somewhat angry as she approached the conference table with me. I greeted her warmly and was ready to praise Steadman's academic abilities. However, she immediately told me all that was wrong with his behavior.

"He's always in trouble at home," she said. "He won't do his chores, and he runs away from me when I try to catch him."

She continued: "He's been in trouble more times at school, too. Fights on the playground, and not doing his work are just some of them."

"That principal blames him for everything!" she huffed. "If I knew where his father was I'd send him to his father."

How sad, I thought. Here is this wonderfully intelligent young man, whom I hoped could be president some day, or at least be a college graduate ranking *summa cum laude*, and his father was missing and his mother was angry. Deep inside I felt anger at that father who abandoned his son. These stories are the harsh reality of neglect. The father was missing so much by not being with this young man and seeing what he could accomplish.

---

solutionsforamerica.org/healthyfam/parent-education. July, 2010

"He works very hard in school. He's a strong leader in our class, and I enjoy his work and efforts." I smiled at her. "You are a smart lady," I said, after all, I was thinking she must be to have this child. "I know you are, because you have such a smart boy."

She smiled, finally, and I hoped that I had made a little inroad into our working together. I learned that she was mad at the principal, mad at the school, and mad at Steadman, all in the same conference. It was odd to me that she felt mad at the school, when she really felt the same way as the principal—exasperated by his actions. All of the negative problems happened before he entered my classroom; I had talked to her on the phone and not once had I mentioned any poor behavior on this student's part. It was so odd to me that she couldn't accept the fact that perhaps he was enjoying school, achieving good grades, and becoming more mature.

The African-American culture, as I mentioned earlier, was matriarchal, and she wanted to be in control. Steadman was determined to control his own destiny, and I hoped it would be the right path. He needed to have some power and learn to make decisions based on choices that were good, not based on demands put upon him by a ruling hand. I felt his success in the classroom centered on his realization that he could make good choices, and he could come to good conclusions on his own power. I wanted a shiny future for Steadman, so I wanted a good relationship with his mother as well.

Much to my excitement, I had about a 60% rate of attendance at conferences, and that was as good as I had expected. In my previous schools I regularly had 100% attendance, but the 60% rate seemed to match the office's expectation, so I was satisfied.

No one came from Mikayle's family.

Chapter Nine

Parenting

In all of the years that I taught, I never found a parent who didn't love his or her children. However, the ability to guide and direct, or to even show that love, as in Steadman's mother's situation, was often the stumbling block to a good relationship and an equally good home environment.

"They act better at school than at home," a parent might comment to me. The important question is why that happens, and the answers often fall far out of the range of my ability to address or remedy them. Absent parents (whether due to long work hours or prison sentences), crowded houses, and little income for even basic necessities—all these things can have a negative impact on a child's behavior. School can provide a welcome haven from the chaos of an impoverished home life.

If parents seek counsel, I am glad to advise and work with them. The parents, however, usually don't ask. It is easy to wonder if anyone, especially me, is up to the task of changing the course of the lives of some of the students in our care for this one small portion of their lives.

Having a good balance of communication and restrictions

isn't easy. Giving children limits is one thing, but knowing how to hold children to those limits in a kind and loving way can be difficult, especially in the inner-city environment. Harshness, yelling, making threats, intimidation, hitting, and abusive language don't really cover the job. Rather, they cause alienation and shattered relationships. Moreover, often these young parents had no strong role models of their own to learn from, and good parenting classes weren't always available or heavily attended.

Physical discipline is often the biggest hurdle to overcome. There is a lot of research on spanking as a form of consequence for children. This is an individual choice, as I mentioned earlier; it isn't the choice I would make within my experience with children. It is a choice that has been used in schools and still is in many states, especially in the South. It has waxed and waned over time, statistically, and there are data both supporting it and defaming its effects.[10]

In one school in which I taught, our counselor offered parenting classes once a week each quarter of the school year. Only the parents who didn't need the counseling came.

Many factors limit the effectiveness of parent education. Here are just a few that I can support from experience:

(1) Cultural responses to discipline: The belief about how to discipline children is deeply placed, often subconscious, and not easily changed. How one was treated as a child, even though it may have been a hated method, becomes ingrained. Under stress, parents rely on familiar methods learned through their own experience from their parents— even when they have read, been taught, or somehow

---

10 "Corporal Punishment in U.S. Schools." By C. Farrell . World Corporal Punishment Research. www.corpun.com, July, 2010

learned new parenting skills and wanted to change their behavior. Yelling, hitting, and spanking in anger are all extremely damaging to children if repeated frequently over time, in my opinion.

(2) Refusal to accept help: In the inner-city community, as in other high-poverty areas, there is a negative reaction to help being given. Parents often have had bad experiences with social services providers and have felt let down. They develop a deep distrust of people whom they view as authority figures, and in turn refuse to accept offers of support and help.

(3) Family stress: Stressors are a huge block to good parenting. If parents are struggling just to survive, they often have no time or energy to cope with anything else. Drug and alcohol abuse, sickness, lack of job security, and not enough money to live on are all paramount stressors in these homes.[11]

---

11 IBID

Chapter Ten

My Life, Revisited

None of my early life was easy. I can remember lying in bed at night hearing my father stagger in drunk.

"You're drunk again," rang my mother's voice clearly through the shallow wall of the bedroom I shared with my siblings.

My father's mumbled reply was not understandable to me.

"Go to bed," my mother said. "You have to look for work tomorrow. We don't have the money for rent."

Oh no! I thought. *Where will we live?* I was eight years old at the time. We had only been in this house a month. It was already our third move since the beginning of school. Getting into the neighborhood school was difficult for me this time. The principal had stuck a book in front of me.

"Have you read this book?" she asked.

In those days the books were all the same series, the Dick and Jane series from Scott Foresman Publishing Company, and she wanted me to pick out the last book I had read.

Feeling timid and unsure of myself, I replied, "I don't think so."

Because of my reticence, I ended up in a grade where the teacher praised me all morning for reading so well and being such a good student. To my horror, she announced what good second graders we were. I knew I was supposed to be in third grade, not second. I ran home for lunch in deep distress.

As I recall this incident, I really wonder why they didn't just ask me what grade I was in from the start. That would have made the selection process a quick one. I guess reading was the key to grade placement, rather than my age, which was clearly on the registration form my mother filled in for the office. This whole experience taught me a bit about adjusting to new situations.

"They put me in second grade!" I shouted as I ran through the door.

My mom responded quickly, walking back to school with me after lunch and making sure I was in the correct classroom. All of this made for a stressful entry into a new and kind of rough school. We were on the south side of Billings, Montana, and this was the "wrong side of the tracks" in those days. Whatever happened at home, I was sure I didn't want to change schools again.

I thought about my school, as I was lying on the top of some logs. I felt helpless. In church I had learned to do penance as I prayed, and I thought if I did a penance, maybe somehow my prayers would be heard. I had gotten out of bed and found my brother's log truck. This was in response to hearing my parents talking in the kitchen. His truck had about ten logs, each only about one-half inch in diameter, so I put all ten of them in bed and laid down on them. It certainly was a penance to me as a small child. It was pretty uncomfortable.

I have a clear memory of those days, and so I felt like I could understand the lives my students led in some of their difficult situations. I could empathize with the situations the parents found themselves in, and if they confided in me, perhaps I could be of help. The students in alcoholic families always try to figure out why. They feel powerless and unsure of who caused the dysfunction in their environment. Mostly we, as children of alcoholics, blame ourselves in some way. I remember praying, *Is it my fault in any way that my father drinks? What else can I do to help make things better?* I loved my father and somehow always wanted to protect him. I followed him around and even climbed on the roof once with him when he was trying to fix our TV antenna. I guess I thought if he started to fall, I could catch him.

I found that if one parent was stable, children didn't feel so helpless. If both parents were drinking, or in prison, it was difficult to cope. This was true in my situation: my mother kept us all together. She saw to it that we didn't miss much school by helping us fill in gaps in our learning if one school had taught a skill prior to our entry.

In one third-grade class I attended the students were already writing cursive. In those days, it was a separate subject. The teacher saw that I was still just printing. "Just connect each letter," she said, and demonstrated it by holding my hand and connecting my printed letters to make a word. My cursive was pretty vertical for a while until I learned how to slant the letters; it was clear that I wasn't as advanced as the rest of the class. I hated feeling like I was behind the other students.

When I needed help, sometimes I would try to involve my father—just desperately hoping my father would spend time with me. "Dad, will you help me with long division?" I asked. He was always kind to me, and there were many good times with him in my memory as well as bad times. He taught us Irish songs and sang when he had his good days.

"Sure," he said, and he sat down at the kitchen table

with me. Everyone else in the class seemed to know how to do long division, and it was a baffling maze to me, because I missed the beginning instruction of it during one of our moves. Amazingly, my father made it all clear. In one evening he helped me understand how easy it really was, because math was usually not hard for me—I liked figuring out how to get answers.

Chapter Eleven

DARE Officers

One of my favorite people to help over my teaching years was the DARE (Drug Abuse Resistance Education) Officer who taught my fifth graders. The DARE Officer usually came during the fall of the year and gave a weekly lesson to help children understand how to say no to drugs, alcohol, and cigarettes, and how to handle other issues they might encounter via peer pressure. My students in the inner city were very much in need of that program. They were bright and eager, and participated in the interactive program well. They acted out scenarios of being pressured, wrote in their notebooks, and answered all of the questions with help. That isn't to say, of course, that they were always attentive; I usually walked up and down the aisles to redirect their attention to the lesson at hand.

Many officers I encountered were not terribly capable of holding a group's attention, because they weren't trained to do so. After all, that wasn't their main job. They were usually eager to get advice from me and I helped when I could. The officer during my fall at Rosa Parks, however, was great. He did as well as any I had seen at keeping the kids motivated and focused. He was young and on the ball as far as getting to know my students, even spending time with them at recess, but it was still hard to keep their concentration on the program, no matter how much fun it was.

And frankly, the DARE program tried to make the lessons fun. I liked the curriculum. It had many opportunities for children to role-play what they would do under peer pressure to smoke, or drink, or even use drugs. I didn't know if any of the information was sinking in, despite the students reiterating it and acting it out as if they really understood what to do. I knew that many of them could still fall into the hands of the tempters that were in every neighborhood. Still, I hoped the program would change some attitudes.

The DARE lesson lasted one hour and continued for a few weeks into the year. After I retired, the DARE program was dropped from curriculums.[12] I was sad to hear that. Statistically, I guess, it hadn't changed the rate of drug or alcohol use. To me, though, that wasn't its only purpose. I often wonder if statistics tell the whole story. Perhaps everyone who comes into our lives affects us in some way; I hope that is true. Yet I have always questioned how we are formed. What has the strongest influence in our lives and of course, in the lives of these precious children? I think the DARE program was a good contributor to providing a means of control in the lives of some students. It gave the children an opportunity to know a police officer in person. They interacted, laughed together, and received praise from this kindly person. For my inner-city students, whose knowledge of police officers often came from hearing parents speak ill of them, just knowing that policemen were human and real people was worth its weight in gold.

---

12   Emmet, SusanR. Ringwalt, Christopher. Fleweeling, Robert L. "Meta Analysis of Project Dare. Ajph.aphapublications.org.

One day during the DARE lesson, the principal walked into the room with a group of visitors from Japan. These folks were visiting the DARE program to see how it worked and if it would or could be successful in their schools. Evidently drugs were an issue, even though the Japanese schools were highly structured and quite determined to be solely academic. I was impressed that they were interested and invited them to look over the material and listen and learn about the program. My students were also glad to have visitors who were interested in what they were doing.

When I think of the influences in my life, I know that there have been many. My difficult childhood made me work harder for everything that I had. My mother's inability to go to college was such a negative influence for her that I wanted to be sure that I was able to change my life by increasing my education. College enhanced me. The power of a broader knowledge base widened my perspectives.

Many of the teachers I had throughout my lifetime influenced me in the areas of trust and encouragement. My high school English teacher went the extra mile in her concern for my well-being. She had a son who was in the mental institution in which my father was housed during my high school years, and she took me there to visit him. It was a windy autumn day, and as I was leaving my father asked me to convince my mother to let him come home. Tears came to my eyes as he lifted his collar, turned, and walked away through the blowing leaves. At that moment, I feared I might never see him again. My teacher counseled me and worked to lift my spirits. When I got married, knowing I had no resources, she bought me a beautiful trousseau. Perhaps many of us can point to teacher who showed caring, understanding, and love far beyond just the classroom setting; after all, teachers have big hearts.

My husband has a strong sense of honor and good

character traits, such as honesty and empathy for others, and he is someone I admire and emulate. He always takes the high road, never putting people down or gossiping about them. My children are the same. Being surrounded by a positive attitude has helped me shift out of a down mood many times over many years. I know that the students I taught can be influenced by their positive experiences.

Besides the DARE program, mentoring for children in the inner city consisted of Big Brother/Big Sister programs, gymnasiums open and supervised after school, and outside homework help in after-school programs. Rosa Parks offered an extended day to staff programs in the areas of science and the arts. This gave the students a lot of opportunity to be supervised at times when they might have been alone.

Chapter Twelve

Working Hard

One of the hardest subjects to teach is writing. When I was at Rosa Parks, the state test involved a writing exam, and the scores from previous years were not good. I wanted to provide an opportunity for students to learn how to express themselves through the written word as well as the spoken, which they were already good at doing. We began with free writing: putting anything on paper that popped into their minds for three minutes. "Writing is just talk written down," I said to ease their worries. It wasn't easy for many of them to do, but we kept at it until it got easier. "Write, write, write," I encouraged, with my stopwatch in hand.

Once they felt the freedom of doing that, we advanced to technique and organization. I inspired them with examples from prize-winning stories that elementary school children had written. I obtained those from different textbook companies that ran contests for all grade levels of elementary school. We wrote daily in some form, and I began to see progress.

Mia came into the classroom one morning with an idea for a story. She sat down and started writing on her own. I looked around; she was the only one doing that, but I was glad that at least someone was feeling good about writing that day. Steadman raised his hand and wanted to get started on our usual beginning of the day. I was hesitant to interrupt Mia, but I knew that the rest of the class needed to begin, so we began.

"O.K.," I said, with much excitement. "This seems like a good day to write. It's October, and Halloween is on its way. Spooky stories are a lot of fun, so let's see if we can start by writing a short paragraph together." I went to the board, anxious to begin. Then I turned around and we started to brainstorm what makes a story scary. Hands flew into the air across the room.

"Someone dies, and so everyone is scared," came a voice from the back.

"I'm sure that's true," I replied. "What other things make you scared?"

"I woke up in the middle of the night and there were sirens everywhere."

"I saw someone shot and the blood was all over the sidewalk."

I paused before asking, "How many of you have seen guns in your neighborhood?"

Every hand went up in the classroom. We talked about what helps them feel safer when that happens. I was beginning to be appalled at all that they had to encounter.

"I run and get under the bed," Mia said

"My favorite spot is my closet," LaMar added.

"It doesn't scare me anymore," shrugged Tyrell.

I started to backtrack a bit and tried to veer the discussion back to spooky stories. They are more fun than reality. We want to entertain when we scare, not have our readers too frightened by what they read. My students' lives involved real fear—fear I could only imagine, because it had never happened in my neighborhood.

We brainstormed words that would help them with their stories and possible topics. Pretty soon, we had made a list of ideas. Finally, I wanted them to decide where the limits were on stories that we wanted to read to small children. By the end of our discussion, we began to get reasonable ideas for sharing with small children. We concluded that children could be scared as long as they feel safe and not threatened by our stories. We decided that we were going to invite the first grade class to join us later in the month when our stories were completed.

We talked about illustrations and what would be fun to include in their final writings. I was excited about their enthusiasm, so the project seemed to be a fitting assignment for the children in my class. It would take us at least two weeks to get to our final project, and I was ready to give them time each day in class.

Next we decided to build a haunted house in the corner of our room, enveloping a small corner with black plastic and spooky ideas. All of the children contributed ideas. We laid out our plans on the board in four columns. The first column told what we needed in supplies. The second column showed who would bring those supplies. The third showed who would be responsible for each job. Finally, the fourth column contained a list of what could go wrong. The list was pretty long in this column, and the children were learning how to make plans in their own lives. At least that was my intention! If we thought about what could go wrong, perhaps we could prevent it. I was hopeful about that, but I knew the level of excitement the children in my class could generate, and self-control was often hard to maintain.

Halloween finally arrived, and we invited the first-grade

class from Mrs. Lomax's room and each child was given a partner. I was a little nervous about how all of our plans would play out in actuality, but I needn't have worried. Most of the children brought the supplies we needed. I had provided extra treats just in case. The most fun for me, and I think actually for the children, was when they read their spooky stories to the first graders. My students sat happily with their younger partners as they read, showing the illustrations and helping the first graders follow along.

What fun it was to get through that whole activity! We were all exhausted at the end of the day, but we found that because we prepared and knew ahead of time what might go wrong, that we actually didn't have too many bad moments.

Goal Setting is a way to help children in all areas of their lives. This activity can help them in a very methodical and structured way to define what they need to do.

The official steps are:
   (1) **Define** the goal. What are you trying to accomplish?
   (2) **Outline** the steps needed to achieve the goal.
   (3) **Prepare** for possible blocks and things that can go wrong. It's helpful to think about ways to deal with a crisis or a mistake.
   (4) **Set deadlines** for accomplishing your goal. It's important to be sure the goal has a reasonable chance of being achieved.[13]

The room was pretty much a mess after the Halloween project was completed, and the bell rang before it was

---

13 "Setting and Achieving Goals—Grades 5-9. www.goodcharacter. com/BCBC/Goals.html

completely clean, but I still chalked it up as a success, as I put the finishing touches on the room before I left that night. I hoped it would be a memory for all the children involved. I can still feel my exhaustion, however, and I knew that it wasn't my last tired moment.

Chapter Thirteen

Stealing

In November, one of my students lost five dollars. Since we were pretty isolated in our classroom, and nobody had visited that morning, I knew it had to have been taken by someone in my class.

I gathered as much information as I could. I believed firmly in finding out who took anything that was missing. If a child who steals isn't caught, he or she often takes it as a sort of license to do it again. This was true in any school. I was sure that if we stopped that behavior early in life, the children would learn their lessons well. Perhaps I was right, maybe not, but I was determined to try.

I finally narrowed my search to Mia. We talked privately during the noon hour. Knowing that having empathy for others is the first step to stopping injustices towards others, I took that approach when quizzing Mia.

I said, "You know how sad Lamar was when he knew someone took his five dollars? When you saw it on the floor by his desk, did you think of how sad he would be when he knew it was stolen?"

She looked at me sincerely and said, "Mrs. Hilton, when

you find money, you just don't give it back. You just don't do that."

I paused at that revelation. If I never had any money in excess, would I give back money that I found? I knew I somehow had to convince her about the right thing to do.

"If this was your money and you were going to spend it on something important to you, would it make you sad if someone stole it?" She hesitated, so I went on to say, "Put your hand on you heart right now, and tell me what you are feeling inside." She thought for a while.

"I'm feeling sad that I am in trouble," she said.

"That's very honest of you to say," I replied. "Now, what I want for you to do is be honest again with me. Did you take LaMar's money?" She nodded.

"All right, Mia. Now I want to teach you how to feel sad for what you've done, not because you are in trouble, but because you hurt LaMar. I want you to think about LaMar. Tell me if you think that LaMar often has money to spend."

"No," she said, "I know he doesn't."

"All right. He said he got this money by doing a chore for his neighbor. Do you think he worked hard for that five dollars?" She nodded and I could see a tear begin to form in the corner of her eyes. I knew then that she was coming to remorse. A child needs to feel remorse—often producing tears can enable them to make changes. I have seen it happen and know it is vital to their success in changing behavior that could lead them into more serious trouble later in life.

Over the years I have found that a consequence is necessary to help a child learn not to repeat a wrong behavior. I assigned Mia to a program that met on Saturdays and was designed to teach empathy for others, to help them understand the pain they caused someone if they stole from them, or hit them, or caused harm in anyway. Does it work?

Not all the time, but I knew this young lady was smart and from a nice family, so I had great expectations for her future. I wanted her to be a successful adult and I knew we should try all possible approaches to success. I used this "Crime School Program" later in another school in which I taught, when one of my students took money from my student teacher.

How do children build character? They glean information from every source they can, I feel. Empathy, when you think about it, is the basis for good moral behavior. Thinking of others and their needs is a wonderful attribute in all of us; I hope it can be taught. In other schools where I taught after I left the inner city, we began to teach one character trait a month. Empathy was always one of the main ones, as I feel so strongly about teaching others to try to see life from someone else's point of view, not always their own.

Good literature was one of the ways I learned how others feel and how we can relate to people in a positive way. I wanted good literature to be important to the students. With every story I read, I pointed out points of empathy through questioning strategies.

"How do you think Kavik, the Wolf Dog, felt when Charlie One Eye hit him? 'His big hand struck, and with a startled yelp of pain and surprise the pup was knocked rolling.'"[14] I always read this old but cherished book to my upper elementary students. I never wanted a child to hurt a pet and this was a story that taught them empathy for a dog. Statistically, if a child hits an animal, he is more likely to grow up to hit people and a vicious cycle begins. There are many other books that help teach empathy for animals.[15]

---

14 Morey,Walt. *Kavik the Wolf Dog*. Scholastic INC., 1968.
15 "Cruelty Connections," www.pet-abuse.com. September, 2010

The *Shiloh* books by Phyllis Reynolds Naylor are other good animal stories.

Many picture books also provide excellent sources to teach this skill. I used picture books all throughout my teaching career, even for upper-grade children. Here are some resources that I found just by typing in my request on a search engine: *Adventures at Walnut Grove* and *I Double Dare You!* by Dana Lehman; *Priscilla McDoodlenutDoodleMcMae Asks Why?* by Janet Mary Sinke; *Cody's Castle: Encouraging Others (Thinking of Others)* by Gary Bower; and the whole series of *The Berenstain Bears* books. Another book that is useful to teachers during these hard economic times is the book, *Tight Times*, by Barbara Shook Hazen. This is a book about a family whose father lost his job. The list goes on and on. There are teacher resources for using activities and lesson plans, but I have found that literature is such a wonderful teaching tool for leading good lives.

Oddly enough, while we are talking about what literature does for children, one of the best series I found that my inner-city children loved was the *Help Me Be Good* series. They are small books by Joy Berry: *Bad Sport, Being Bossy, Being Bullied, Breaking Promises, Stealing, Teasing,* and some thirty-odd other titles. My pupils wanted to read these books over and over. It surprised and delighted me. I read the stories to them, and they read them again and again on their own. I found that true in other classrooms as well. Sometimes the children in dysfunctional homes are starving for learning how to behave.

One of the plans we had for raising money for our school parties was to have a candy sale after school. We bought candy in bulk and sold it, with the students being the cashiers and sales persons. It was a great success. We did it a few times during the week and made a bit of a profit to go toward "extra" items that we needed for the classroom and eventually for the children's graduation from fifth grade. Unfortunately, our money never quite equaled what we thought it should and we often suspected someone was taking either the candy or the money. How I worried about that. I wanted children to know that if they didn't have money for candy, I would give them a candy treat now and then, but a sense of honesty is truly what I wanted to instill in all of my students. Being honest is hard even for grown-ups who are faced with a confession of wrongdoing. Honesty must be taught at an early age, and reinforced consistently.

Once in a while things went missing from my desk. I always knew that someone was upset at me, because I soon learned that was the way they showed their disfavor with one of my decisions. Often in a couple of days the item was returned. Feelings must have been mended. Somehow I had redeemed myself in their eyes, so I could have my stapler back. This phenomenon was unique to Rosa Parks; I had never experienced it in any other school in which I taught over the years.

Sometimes it is difficult to teach children something they haven't experienced before. If they were taught the concept of revenge by the actions around them, in school or at home, it was difficult to "un"-teach. Perhaps they were upset over too much homework. Or maybe they wanted me to read a story longer, which happened a lot. They loved the story after lunchtime, and they hoped I would read to them all afternoon.

"Has anyone borrowed my stapler?" I would ask, hoping to get it back promptly.

"My scissors are missing," I'd comment. The objects were never found in the room. Backpacks weren't searched in this instance … nothing was. I just learned to trust that the objects would be returned, and they always were. I often thought that maybe the children wanted to use the objects they took, because they didn't think I would willingly lend the items, although I would happily have done so. I didn't explore a motive in this case, as I had too many other pressing problems.

Chapter Fourteen

Rewards

Over many years I worked to obtain my bachelors and masters degrees, and then I attended education classes and workshops yearly to support and enhance my teaching abilities. I have studied all of the approaches to educating children that I thought would help me. I felt those classes were relevant and important to my growth as a teacher. One of the strong techniques advocated in the 1970s was Positive Reinforcement. Many use it today. In fact, getting a paycheck is a form of reward for behavior on the job. That was one of the many supports for using this technique at home and in the classroom. Teachers and parents used gold star charts, M&Ms, and other tokens as rewards for good behavior. I used it myself occasionally for my own children when they were small.

I found that in my inner-city school, positive reinforcement was a particularly prominent technique used. The student body comprised a corps of children who only responded to outward reward, rather than feeling great about having done something considered good behavior. The intrinsic reward just wasn't enough for many of them.

Most teachers in elementary schools had used rewards, often candy, or other desired gifts to promote good behavior. The problem was that the students in this situation got candy far too often. Perhaps they got an M&M for coming inside quietly, or for standing in line. Maybe they got a treat merely for doing their work. These outside motivators only last as long as the piece of candy. By fifth grade, if a reward was mentioned, they simply got angry if they didn't get the reward, whether they did the action to deserve it or not.

I soon learned how ineffective rewards were for changing behavior over time. I certainly saw the damage they could do if overused. I read the book by Alfie Kohn entitled *Punishing with Rewards,* [16] which I found to be such a true account of what was happening in my classroom. I attended an afternoon session with Alfie Kohn as the speaker and thoroughly agreed with his point of view. "Rewards and punishments are both ways of manipulating behavior!" What I truly wanted to see was the children's own sense of right and wrong, and feeling good about their achievements.

The problem with rewards was highlighted when we went to an assembly just before Thanksgiving. Children are so restless before vacation breaks under normal circumstances, and this session proved my point about rewards. The presenters were speaking about sports and handed out three posters for each grade as a raffle-type gift. The children were furious when they returned to the classroom, because they hadn't received one of the posters. I told them to think about it, before they complained too much.

"Why didn't I get one of those posters?" Ebony whined.

"I hate those people," Tyrell said angrily

---

16 Kohn, Alfie. Punishing By Rewards. The Trouble With Gold Stars, Incentive Plans, A;s, Praise and Other Bribes. Boston:Houghton Mifflin, 1993/1999.

"They just wanted to keep them for themselves," Deasia chimed in. "I know they had more."

I looked around. "Did you expect to get a gift when you went to the assembly?" I asked. No one admitted they thought that. "Then why are you so angry because you didn't get one?"

They became silent.

"When you go home every afternoon from school, do you expect to be able to go to the movies?" They laughed, because they hadn't had that happen very often. I went on, "If you go home from school and your mama says, 'I'm going to take you to the movies,' wouldn't that be a wonderful surprise and make you grateful?"

"Yes!" they shouted.

"You would be happy to have such a gift, but you wouldn't expect it all the time, right?" As they nodded, I concluded, "Do you think you could be happy, because some people were lucky, just not you this time?" I didn't convince anyone of that, but by asking questions I prompted them to think a little deeper about their original response.

It was quite difficult to convince these children that what teachers advocated was for their own good. Teachers therefore used every method they could to achieve what they wanted—like quiet classrooms, and lines, and good behavior, completed assignments—things that in more privileged schools would be considered normal classroom conditions. If a piece of candy was a motivator for a while, they used what worked. Was it a good idea? I didn't think so, because by the fifth grade, the students wanted the piece of candy whether they deserved it or not and were angry if they didn't get it. Rewards lost their incentive and meaning. By far the best motivator is an intrinsic desire to learn and achieve; only those motivators that come from within are powerful enough to last a lifetime.

Instead, motivation based on external rewards engenders a feeling of entitlement. "The world owes me something!" This feeling only causes bitterness when life gets hard, and it is ultimately destructive to growth and achievement. Entitlement breeds another unproductive attitude: blaming the teacher or the school when the children themselves have done something wrong. Taking ownership for one's own actions is important to growth and development.

I know that positive reinforcement works for a while, but the long-range results are not very good for children. Knowing this, I found myself left with so few motivating options. I had to build in the desire for good grades and feeling good about how they behaved and how they performed in class. It wasn't easy.

The approach I used was a direct promotion of taking pride in one's own work. When a student received 100% on a paper. I praised him or her, and then asked, "How does it make you feel when you get a grade like that?" I wanted my pupils to stop and think about how they were feeling about doing well.

"Good,' they would say almost universally.

"How hard did you have to work to achieve that grade?" Naturally they wanted to convince me they had worked at their best, so I told them to hold the good feeling inside of them to help them work hard as many times as they could.

"Success breeds success," is my mantra. Find some way that everyone could achieve during the day and help build on that success. If children received all failing grades because their work was not at the grade level just yet, how would they ever work harder? I reviewed with the children over and over until they achieved a level of success that got them above the failing mark. I tried to instill the value of hard work and never giving up.

Chapter Fifteen

Thanksgiving

These were exciting months. My goal was to be sure that the class kept thinking about hard work while at the same time had an activity about which they were enthused and motivated. Their excitement about Thanksgiving and Christmas were no different than any other group of children that I have taught, except this group was even more excitable.

Report cards were coming out, but the children were not as concerned with performance as I wanted them to be. Actually, what my wildest dreams conjured up for all my children was the intrinsic motivation that helps them do their best. Grades are merely a report about whether they reached their goals. This, of course, holds true only when students are sincere about the goals we tried to set in the aftermath of our first conferences. I knew I was idealistic and set some impossible goals for myself, many of which were also passed on to my students. I was realistic about how many I could actually achieve, though, because I didn't count myself as a total failure when many children didn't reach their goals.

I was afraid that the emphasis on achievement took a back seat too often to survival, sociability, and fun. I wanted to make studying more fun and less tedious—which is not always possible, so hard work needs to be acceptable to my students as well. I decided the month's goals were to intersperse academic goals with break times and fun art projects connected with Thanksgiving. As they finished their assignments and brought in their completed homework, we could release a bit of time for finishing some artwork, each time emphasizing how it felt inside to complete what they needed to do. That plan seemed to be working.

Each student was to make a three dimensional replica of the Thanksgiving feast, including the table, chairs, tablecloth, and paper replicas of the meal. They didn't have a lot of experience with the cutting and pasting, since they tended to abuse the supplies (or had done, at the beginning of the year). However, they had learned that if they misused their project supplies, they lost the privilege of their project time until the next day. This was for their first offense. It might take two incidents to get the point across, so they lost three days of project time if they misbehaved again. All was going pretty well until someone poured a whole bottle of Elmer's Glue onto Tyrone's chair. It was easy to find the culprit on that one, though; I just had to check glue bottles. Evidently, Tyrell was extremely angry with Tyrone for some unintended push, or so Tyrone said. According to Tyrell it was intentional. The bell rang, school was over, and I had to line them up for dismissal.

I sat at my desk after scooping up as much glue as possible. Was the day ruined by this incident? At the moment I felt it was, and I was sad. As I sat there, I thought back to the happy voices, and the hard workers who deserved to work on their art projects, and I started to feel a bit better. I decided to go to the store on the way home and buy glue sticks for the rest of the project. Nothing seemed to be able to appease hot tempers at the moment of that temper flaring. Anger causes so much heartache.

We started the next day with a class meeting. Tyrell gave his side of the story and Tyrone gave his. We talked about how the glue on Tyrone's desk got on his clothes before he noticed it. He almost sat down in the middle of that puddle of sticky glue.

I asked Tyrell if he had put Tyrone's name on the class meeting list.

He said, "No, I didn't want to talk about it! He was wrong, and he deserved to be hurt."

"Why did you choose to spill his glue?" I asked.

"It was there, and I just did it!" Tyrell shrugged.

"Tyrone deserved it," added Ebony. "He pushed Tyrell."

Other voices chimed in against Tyrone.

Tyrone was putting his head down and turning red, looking very unhappy.

I opened the discussion to the class. Some started to side with one or the other, but mostly with Tyrell, who was more popular. I had a feeling this would happen, so I began to ask my questions.

"Was the punishment that Tyrell suggested for Tyrone respectful to him?" We talked about how they would feel if they accidentally ran into someone and that person had not given them a chance to explain.

"Even if he did it on purpose, would throwing the glue on his chair help him to change his behavior?" Most of them agreed that it would not.

"Was it related to what he did, if he pushed Tyrell on purpose?"

They all agreed it wasn't. Tyrone said, much to my joy, that he was sorry he pushed the other boy. Tyrell took a little longer to accept the apology, so I delved further: "Do you feel a little bit sad about spoiling our fun at the end of the day?"

I smiled at him, because I wanted him to know he was not a bad person, but that he might have made a mistake. I voiced that feeling. I said the same thing to Tyrone. By this time there was enough silence to hear a pin drop—a very rare occasion.

Tyrell took a deep breath and finally said,

"It's OK, and I'm sorry it happened.

"All right Tyrell, what do you think you should do to help yourself be able to not react in that way again?" He couldn't think of anything so I asked the class to give ideas.

"Maybe he could work for you to pay for the glue."

"Or he could be in charge of the glue and make sure everyone doesn't waste it," Deasia said.

"He could write a story about how he would do it a different way."

I nodded. "Those are all good suggestions. Now we can let Tyrell choose what he thinks would be the consequence that would help him the most to be able not to lose his temper so quickly."

While he was thinking about that, I asked Tyrone what he was going to do to help him not push other people, if it wasn't an accident. The other students raised their hands for suggestions.

"He should take a deep breath before he does anything!"

"Great idea," I replied.

Then something wonderful happened. Mia said, "Since Tyrone has a sore foot, maybe he slipped a little and his push was really accidental. Everyone should think about that before they get mad at him."

Wow! We went from taking sides to actually empathizing! That was a huge step in the right direction. It took a lot of time, but oh how necessary to clear the air, and it certainly set me up for a spirit of thankfulness in the middle of November. I felt that this, rather than a lecture, was a far more beneficial way to add closure to this incident.

I had shifted the thinking to the students. I wanted them to use their minds to find a solution that was agreeable to everyone involved. Coming to consensus isn't always possible, but because Mia made such a positive move toward Tyrone's point of view, it helped to shift the thinking to a fairer assessment of this situation. The rest of the day went well, with no more major incidents. Children with quick tempers can easily do something they'll regret for a long time. Teaching empathy for others is one way to help quell disaster.

Tyrell decided that he would take the job of taking care of the glue as his consequence. He wanted to count the glue sticks each day and make sure they were all in the box at the end of the day. I was satisfied with that choice.

When I taught junior high in another school district, I remember an incident when an eighth grade boy picked up a sixth grade girl and actually dropped her over a stairwell. Amazingly, the sixth grader was not seriously hurt, but I was the first teacher to get to the scene. I calmly asked the older student why he had hurt another person, and he replied that he didn't like her.

I said, "Look at the tears and the fear in her face, and tell me how you feel now."

This abusive boy began to show remorse as he watched the littler girl sobbing and shaking. I gave him the job of protecting her, because she often got teased and mistreated during the breaks. The boy accepted the challenge and at every encounter in the hallways he checked with her about her day; soon, he began to really know this little girl and feel a friendship. He reported to me weekly. This certainly was one successful way to use empathy to help another grow in his ability to feel for another child. Is this a better method than a three-day suspension? I think so, because it actually changes behavior and promotes a lifetime skill.

I would recommend this method of linking offenders with the persons they hurt—*when* you feel the personalities could handle that assignment. It should only be if you see signs of caring within the abuser. Teachers I have worked with seem to have a good sense of character potential. We usually can make good judgments about what would work to help change behavior. Again, I reiterate, teachers need to work within their own personalities when it comes to teaching self-discipline for children. Above all, teachers must listen to children. I feel strongly that children shy away from telling adults about problems, because many adults don't listen carefully to what the child is saying, or they blast them for something immediately without delving into the problem. I am definitely not for siding with a child who has done something wrong, as you can see. All children need consequences for wrong behavior, but it should be dealt out in a humane way with the intention of honoring the dignity of both the offender and the offended. The purpose of the consequence should always be to change behavior, not merely to inflict punishment.

Chapter Sixteen

Art Projects

How different education was when I was growing up—at least when compared with almost all of our modern approaches. Looking back, it seems to me that art education was so stagnant and uncreative. I can remember coloring a large picture of George Washington. We were told exactly what to color each part, and I made a mistake. We were supposed to color the shirt white and his tie blue and I accidentally colored part of his shirt with the blue color. I was horrified. My heart almost stopped beating. I was afraid of my teacher and I didn't want to ask her for another picture to color. I also didn't want to turn one in that was not correctly colored. I folded it up and put it in my pocket rather than turning it in.

The next day the teacher said she was missing one of the pictures, and she called the names of those who had turned their pictures into her. She wanted each of us to stand up as our name was called. I stood up when her head was turned, and I was so frightened that she would find out what I did. I had never gotten into trouble before, and I didn't want to start.

Of course, she discovered I was the one and called my mother, who dug the picture out from under my bed where I had stashed it. I can remember so plainly that she ironed it and we had to both go in and talk to the teacher. What a lesson for me! I was scolded and had to re-do the picture. I didn't ever want the children in my class to be afraid to talk to me about anything that might go wrong in their projects. Certainly, they needed to discuss things with me that worried them.

For me, that experience taught me another important lesson: always be honest. With each lie, I seemed to get deeper in trouble, and I got more scared about what would happen to me. I also felt ashamed of myself as I faced my teacher. Internalizing that feeling helped me to decide to choose honesty over lying. In order to teach my students that lesson, I knew it was important to build a level of trust with them.

I created that tryst by listening rather than scolding. I spent time figuring out how to help them by talking, probing, questioning, and treating them with respect. Honesty was taught in my home, and most children know that telling the truth is important. Fairness is a major issue and needs to be emphasized as a teacher decides on who is right and who is wrong, or if both students are a little bit right and a little bit wrong.

"He's lying!" they say, in accusatory voices, whenever anyone tattles on them.

"That's not fair," they say, when the scale tips ever so slightly in the direction they don't prefer.

Even though I sought to maintain fairness, I also taught that life isn't always fair. Bad things happen for no reason, and we need to learn to roll with what happens. None of this can be taught in a year's time.

In one of the schools in which I was employed, the

counselor ran a wonderful program to train children to solve problems with each other. Students role-played common incidents that happened on the playground or in the classroom during a workshop. they learned how to listen to both sides of the problems; then they offered solutions . Our counselor was so successful at training and working with the children that when I was out at recess, if children had a problem, they would come running to me and stand in front of me so I could hear them mediate their issue. One would tell his or her side, then the other, and soon they decided on a solution and ran off to play. I hadn't even said a word to help them; they did it all. Mediation sessions were available to them on a certain day of each week, if it couldn't be solved before then.

The Thanksgiving feast dioramas were coming together for many of the students, but it was such a struggle for some. Small motor skills were hard for half of the fifth graders, and I suggested that as students finished, they would help those who hadn't been able to complete the project. The feasts they made had a little soul food in them—collard greens and black-eyed peas graced some of the tables—and I was learning more and more about the culture. We took pictures and had fun thinking of their Thanksgiving in miniature. It was a good project.

Chapter Seventeen

Kwanzaa

Among all the new experiences I had at Rosa Parks, nothing was as new to me as Kwanzaa.[17] I had not heard much about it, even though it was a holiday initiated in 1966 by Dr. Karenga. I was clueless. I listened in at the meeting after school on the first school day in December. I was pretty fascinated by how the faculty planned the celebration. I said I would help when and where I could, but I was at the meeting to learn as much as I could about this interesting celebration. I discovered that it is celebrated during the week between Christmas and New Year's, and we were going to emphasize the seven principles throughout the month.

The first principle is unity (*umoja*). One should strive for and maintain unity among the family, community, nation, and races. We tried to become a community in one year's time in the classroom by helping each other, learning together, and talking through our problems.

Kujichagulia means self-determination, and represents

---

17   KWANZAA. The First Fruit Celebration.www.afrocentricnews.
com

the second principle. This is such an important concept. Peer pressure or gang pressure eats us up sometimes—even adults who should have learned their lessons early in life, but so often don't. To have self-determination is to make your own choices based on your own inner thoughts and feelings. Hopefully those feelings make your stronger and a contributing member of society.

Third comes *ujima*, a term for collective work and responsibility. This is a very important quality for bringing a classroom together. Understanding each other's problems and trying to help is what makes up a community. The class meetings are a wonderful example of trying to build community through careful talking and solving problems. (It's a lifetime adventure!)

Ujamaa is about cooperative economics—making the community supported by shops and businesses. Dr. Karenga said that these fourth and fifth principles will help "to make our collective vocation the building and developing of our community in order to restore our people to their traditional greatness." So much has happened to the African-American community in our nation. None of us can be proud of what happened to an intelligent and talented race of people during the sad period of our history that involved slavery. I am forever thankful that opportunities exist today for all people.

One way that the principle of ujamaa runs through the entire year comes toward the end of the year, when the business community sends a representative of an organization they run to teach kids about business. The organization's name is Junior Achievement and is still active in today's schools. They spend several weeks teaching our students about how profit and loss affect business, and how businesses make profits and succeed. Our candy sales after school were a beginning in teaching this aspect of life to the children.

Kumbaa, creativity, is sixth—to look for ways to beautify the community and make it better than it is in the present. Finally, *imani* is faith to know how capable the black race is. We certainly see that in all avenues of society today, where African-American people show their talents, intelligence, athleticism, and ability, at all levels. I was proud of every achievement each child was making and what potential they had to succeed.

The ceremony occurred on the day before Christmas break. It was simple and lovely, with many children giving a memorized but heartfelt explanation of each principle. Each classroom had representatives that participated. It was a great way to incorporate learning into a fun-filled holiday. I felt that the learning associated with Kwanzaa was a helpful way to build a sense of community involvement.

We engaged in many other activities for the holiday season, including making Christmas-related crafts and art projects. Learning to be creative is a process that soothes the soul. I could always tell when my class was immersed in a right brain project: the room got very still and totally quiet. It was a rare and lovely thing, because I knew that it also was a gift to children. The gift was the total feeling of calm immersion into a sense of achievement of something tangible and beautiful. The hustle and bustle of holidays is not always soothing—just enter any store during that time. I used soft music in the background while the children worked, to help create a sense of calmness that could extend into each child.

At our Christmas party, we repeated our story building exercise by writing a Christmas story to share with our first-grade buddies. What fun we had creating a good story with Christmas feeling and a happy ending. I brought candy canes, and after the children read their stories, they all ate the candy canes with their buddies. They were proud to show off the ornaments we made for our Christmas tree; the activity was such a successful ending before our Christmas break.

Chapter Eighteen

Christmas Vacation

A two-week break to regroup and refresh! Do all professions need a break? I think so, but for teachers and children— particularly in that inner-city world in which I taught—it can be essential. When I first started teaching, we only had a week, sometimes a bit longer depending on how the holidays fell that year. But with today's extreme scheduling and high stress, we needed two weeks. Less, and the children returned to school tired and not able to study and learn.

I think we all need fresh starts periodically in the year.

How do teachers use the break? For me, it was a time not to get up at 5:00 a.m., struggle with traffic, plan daily lessons, and face the rigorous schedule of the day. It didn't mean not thinking about school, but it did mean not thinking about school every minute of the day and night.

My goal for the break was to work on the curriculum for the remainder of the year. I needed to set up the units of study geared to this group of children, knowing their wants and needs better now than I did at the beginning of the year. This break gave me some time to immerse myself in the units and tweak them for each student.

Teaching to my fastest student to make sure he or she was challenged at the same time as supporting those who were not quite there yet was a constant challenge. It required consistent testing to be sure of what everyone knew and how each child was progressing in all subjects. Besides the rigor of daily study, there was the need to motivate in ways that were unique, challenging, and fun for children, and helped them feel successful.

I spent a lot of time choosing the next books we would read. I also worked out the vocabulary lists and two or three different ways to approach learning vocabulary. Most of my students were auditory learners, so I made tapes for them; I planned to have a listening center with my voice reading the chapter again.

In one hour of reading time, I would start with the whole group. We read both silently and out loud, so everyone could follow the gist of the day's story. This lasted about twenty minutes. During that time I would probe for how well the students comprehended the story. After that, I would send some who needed the practice to listen to the tapes of the story again.

I would give the children who had greater comprehension some questions related to the story, or a writing assignment, using the new vocabulary. If they finished that, they could read another book that was free reading while I met with a skill group of children who needed my guidance on practicing words and comprehension ideas from our book. When I finished with them, I would rotate to free reading of books that would give practice for fluency.

There are many methods for helping children increase speed in reading. I often shadow read with children, so they must keep up the pace with me. We would read together, so they would learn expression and fluency. Repetition is not dull or boring for children. It gives them a feeling of power to read with a fluency they don't have when starting a new book, so choosing easier reading when they are independent is important to their success.

Math is such a fascinating array of systems. I was working on how I could teach them the wonderful realities of "the nines." I love the fact that when you multiply any number times nine you can add the digits of the answer and they equal nine.

Mental math was a daily session, to help the students compute, so they could feel proud of getting faster and better at computation. We did these mental math sessions in the first fifteen minutes at the beginning of math time. Mental math skills are so important. I wanted the children to be able to figure in their minds how to compute simple problems like 10% of fifty. I taught them simple tricks, like if you are adding 9+7 you can either memorize that it is sixteen, or learn to add 1 to nine to make 10 and then subtract the 1 from 7 to make six. We practiced how to divide by breaking up the numbers: 126 divided by 3 is the same as cutting up 126 into 12 and 6; 12 divided by 3 is 4 and 6 divided by 3 is 2, so the answer is 42. I put the problems on transparencies and we worked our way through a book entitled, *Mental Math in the Middle Grades*.[18] I also used the approach of presenting to the whole class and practicing with small groups. We cycled through math skills, reviewing often.

My goals for the next semester were to create more fun math projects to assure their love of math. It was a tall order! I could feel that my students were progressing well in math, but I needed more time. While they were progressing at a steady rate, they were still far behind on the basic skills

---

18 Hope, Jack A., Reys, Barbara J, and Reys, Rober E. <u>Mental Math in the Middle Grades</u>. Dale Seymour Publications, 1987.

compared to other students I had taught in fifth grade. I was hoping to make them more confident learners in math.

My husband and I loved trying to find ways to make life better for our children in the inner city. My husband said that maybe we should get them out of the city for a weekend. During the break we were brainstorming how to do just that. We pondered opportunities and finally came up with a plan that we thought would work. It would take some calling, but we were going to give it a try.

We lived about forty-five minutes from the Oregon coast. In the city, the children mostly saw concrete around them, but a drive to the coast would reveal beautiful green fields and lovely water vistas. I knew that by now the parents had begun to trust me, so I could approach them with the beach trip idea. We planned to take groups of four each trip. We would spend time in Seaside, and then return to our home for dinner and back to their homes by 8:00 p.m. I knew it would take many hours to set up and about six weekends of Saturdays to include every child.

We laid out our plans; I got the notes ready to send home, and set up a tentative schedule. Weekends in February, March and April would be the best months to do the traveling, since the weather would be getting better by then. I thought I would start with the parent, grandparent, or caregiver for the children that I knew best and hope that the others would hear how much fun the students were having. That way they would work on getting permission to take the Saturday adventure! All in all, the Christmas break seemed productive to me, and I was ready when the first day's bell rang for school to start.

Chapter Nineteen

January

Cold, rainy, gloomy gray was the way the day began. I edged my way onto the bridge as two lanes ballooned into four and traffic came at me from both sides. It was always difficult for me to edge my way into the lane I needed. Someone tried to get into my lane, and as I motioned to let him in, he misunderstood me and started to make a rude gesture, but suddenly recognized that I was being polite and quickly changed it to a wave. *Human nature*, I thought. Why is our first response often the wrong conclusion about someone's motive?

I knew that small things could ruin a day for people; they most certainly could set children off on a low point if something happened to them at home, on the playground, or even as they lined up for going into class. Just as a gesture in traffic could set my day off to a poor start, many small things could make children sad or angry.

I also remembered my humble beginnings as a driver. I learned to drive in a small town in Montana. We had 800 people and no traffic light, with very little traffic. What a change my life had experienced over the many years since then. Perhaps we never lose our initial perception of certain things; mine said that driving should always be without many other cars on the road in my way! I chuckled at the absurdity of that statement. The inner city was a crowded mass of people and cars were in my way all the time as I entered the busy roadways leading to school.

I also reminisced a bit about something fun that had happened to us as my husband was coming out of a football stadium in a nearby town. He let a group of young high school kids go in front of him to get into the crowded lane of traffic. As we edged our way to a halt, because no one was moving, the young driver got out and brought back a quarter. With a chuckle he said he always paid when someone let him into a lane of traffic. My husband sat in the traffic a while as we edged forward, and then he jumped out and handed the boy a dime. He said, " I only charge 15 cents for doing that!" We all enjoyed the interchange, and it has been a fun family story to recall over the years.

I managed to get to school in the pouring rain. The parking lot was empty, because it was still so early. Even though my lesson plans were ready, I wanted to set up stations, have papers ready for action, and prepare the overhead projector—all of which I preferred to do before the students arrived. I was hoping my room would be warm, even though I knew it probably wouldn't be at that early hour. However, the janitor knew my schedule by now, so as I walked into the front door he said, "I turned your heat on, and it should be nice and warm for you!"

After thanking him profusely, I inquired about his vacation time, and he said he spent the days waxing the floor and getting everything ready for the return of the children. My husband, as an administrator, always thought janitors were a special group of workers. Most of them take great pride in their jobs, and I totally agreed that Charles was at the top of the ladder in terms of care and treatment of the school.

I asked him where they had put the projectors over the holiday and he pointed me in the right direction. "Thanks so much again, Charles! You have started my day out so well by giving me a warm and cozy place to go." I procured the projector and headed to my room to drop off my bag, the machine, and to grab the things I needed to copy for the day.

Now I had to face the copy machine, which I had hoped had been repaired during the holiday as well, and with luck I could be in my room by 7:00 to go back over my plans and make sure everything was in place. The copy machine worked better than before the holiday, and since I was the first to use it, my copy job finished quickly.

The room felt cozy and reassuring as I sat to think my way through the day. I was hoping the children would come back refreshed and eager to learn and be together. Usually in my other school experiences, students were happy to see each other and catch up on how everyone enjoyed the holidays. I hoped that was the case in this new environment, but I wasn't prepared for the first assault of the day. I went outside.

I watched carefully during the last few minutes before the bell rang. The playground was noisy and busy. Greetings weren't always cordial, and I saw a fight start to form. As quickly as possible I stepped in and found two boys very angry—and it was only 8:30 on day one of the new semester. Evidently the basketball courts were crowded and they were sparring to get the ball away from each other. As soon as I arrived they turned, the bell rang, and they started toward their line.

We began by talking about the most fun they had during the break. Their chatter provided a great incentive to write an interesting essay about their vacations. I pointed out the steps to making everyone understand how they felt through the written word. This was a well-used topic among teachers, but I gave it a twist. "You can pretend you did anything or went anywhere you wanted to go, Use you imagination and create a great vacation story."

"Put the main points you want to express in your opening statement and then take each point and make a full paragraph about it," I instructed. They got to work and the room was deep into a very quiet session of writing. I knew that the test for writing was coming in the beginning of March, and we had a long way to go to improve their writing skills. I used every opportunity I could to help.

The best way to teach this important skill was by demonstrating. I would write a simple sentence on the board like, "Today was a good day." Then I'd ask for four other sentences that explained what made the day good. I used easy beginning sentences. Then, as they were writing their own essays, I would help each one as needed and go over the results with them. I tried to conference throughout the writing to assist with crafting their broad opening sentence and then the detail sentences.[19]

I had taken a workshop on "Power Writing," which was a very precise approach to writing in essay form. I referenced it above. Not only was it effective in simplifying the form, but it also helped teach transitional words that the children could use. Writing is a difficult skill that is easier for some children than others. For those who struggled, it was better to teach a method that was sequential and learned.

One of the hard parts of writing for every teacher is how long it takes to correct the papers. I usually tried

---

19 Poulton, Shirley. Power Writing Plus: Teach the Traits of Effective Writing. Grand Haven MI:C&C Graphics Publishing, 2004.

to meet with each child or have two children at my side conferencing, but the time constraints made completing the task very difficult during school time. I took home the papers that I couldn't complete in class. The next day it was faster to conference when I had already highlighted the error points. This seemed to help more than just handing a paper back to them with corrections on it. In most of the classrooms I had taught, I grouped children so they could read their story to each other. In this setting, however, the children were afraid to share their stories and lacked the self-confidence to read in front of their peers. I was hoping that we could gradually change that, and that they would be proud to share.

One thing that writing can do for children is giving them a venue for expressing their feelings. Sitting in a quiet place that was special to them and writing out how they felt—mad, sad, happy, afraid—had a calming effect for them. In fact, one of the stories I always liked them to write about was if they had a special, secret place where they could go and be alone to do their thinking.

In all of the classrooms I taught, when I introduced this writing topic, every child could tell me about their special place. Don't we all have one where we feel special, alone, and calm?

"My closet back behind the clothes is my favorite place," Deasia volunteered. "No one can find me when I'm in there, and it is mostly quiet."

"If I walk down the block, there is an empty lot that has an old shed. I sit behind it and no one knows I'm there," added Tyrell.

Steadman said, "I have a tree that I climb. I sit on the third highest branch and I hide. I can look at the sky and clouds and think."

"Mine is in our basement, behind the hot water heater. I lay a blanket there and do my thinking," added Mia.

Writing about their special places made for a good topic that everyone in the class could relate to and enjoy. I was happy with their continuing progress in writing.

Chapter Twenty

More Hard Work

The task of finding heroes for children changed over my lifetime. It used to be that movie stars were heroes in my eyes, but in today's world that is often shattered by media's exposure of their every move. The same thing is true of sports figures. Though children looked up to their accomplishments, they certainly saw their flaws, which were in the news more than their athletic prowess. I finally decided that the best heroes for children could be found in literature.

Reading has always helped me escape the cares of the day for a while and relieves the worries of the moment, as I immerse myself into the pages of a good book. I hoped my love of reading would excite and encourage children to love reading as well.

We began to read *Bridge to Terabithia* by Katherine Patterson. This Newberry Book Award winner shows how true friendship develops and shows how two friends can create a world in which to play. "Together Jess, the narrator and main character, and Leslie, his new-found friend, created Terabithia, a magical kingdom in the woods where the two of them reign as king and queen and their imaginations set the only limits. Leslie teaches Jess a strength and courage that he never had before he met her."[20]

I was beginning to be excited by their reactions to parts of the story. They loved the opening race scene where Jess thinks he is the fastest runner in the school. Leslie speeds by him. She is the new girl in his grade, and who would ever think a girl could outrun the fastest boy in the school? Shattering bias and extolling virtues is all part of the thinking involved in this good book. My children looked forward to reading time, and that lifted my spirits and helped me feel like today was a good day.

One thing I always liked to do after reading a book that students were so engaged in was to show a film of the movie. After hours of reading and my teaching them to picture in their minds what the characters looked like and how the story looked linked with their feelings about it, we saw the movie. The movie invariably was never liked as well as the pictures they put in their own minds as they read. That's why I showed the movie; I wanted them to prefer active reading and thinking to the passive effort it took to just watch a story.

January continued with a pattern of hard work in the morning and less ability to concentrate in the afternoon. Again we graphed their sleep patterns during math instruction. Would I ever convince them that going to bed at 11:00 p.m. was not going to help them concentrate through a whole day's work?

"Let's look at your daily graphs. Our bar graphs show the blue color bar as the amount of sleep time you need each night. The red bar shows how much you are getting when you go to bed at 11:00 p.m. What is the difference?"

---

20 Paterson, Katherine. Bridge to Terebithia, Harper Collins, 1977

Steadman raised his hand. "Three hours," he said.

"Now let's look at the line graphs for your whole week. Add up the amount of hours you lose of sleep through the entire week."

"Is that why we get tired?" asked LaMar

"What do you think?" I responded.

"What are some things you can do to make yourself go to bed earlier?"

"Turn off the T.V.," said Ebony. "But Grandma watches *The Late Show* and it keeps me up."

Mia chimed in with, "The music at my house is too loud for me to go to sleep."

"What can you do about that? I asked.

I called parents again and checked in on what was happening in the home, hoping to remind them how important a good night's sleep was to a successful school day. I know that long hours at their jobs or looking for employment made their days hectic, and I didn't want to undermine that achievement in any way. I just wanted to encourage participation in the success of their children. Often homes were busy and loud, so concentrating on getting to sleep was a huge effort.

The testing program at that time just included writing, reading, and math. The hardest part of the testing was making sure that the children understood the vocabulary of the directions on the test. Vocabulary was an important part of instruction; we dealt with it constantly. There was a list of ten words at the beginning of each week that students needed to learn to define. We worked and practiced daily, along with spelling. I encouraged them to use the words we studied in their writing. Reading and writing a lot helped them to improve their grasp of new words as much as time would allow. Pausing in reading to them, I asked about the meaning of words I had just said. Without vocabulary knowledge it was an isolated world. Tests happened each Friday. I found that my students were slowly but surely improving their skills.

As I mentioned before, I tried always to teach to the fastest learner and then review and re-teach to each small group. I know that children learn from each other, and that higher achievers can be a huge boost to students who are learning a skill. Mixing all levels together greatly enhances self-concept and the speed of learning. This month, as usual, I formed a small skills group to help those who were struggling with the words to read in the story. Small groups and even one-on-one conferences helped those who were behind in their skills. There wasn't enough time in the day to reach all of the needs, but I worked long and hard. Recess time provided a break we *all* needed. Ms. Lanikin had consented to my plan to take my students out to recess under my direct supervision. I was very grateful for that. The break was important to them.

The concentration level of my students seemed to wax and wane. They needed more rest breaks and change of subjects than most fifth graders I had worked with prior to this school. I needed to adjust expectations so that I didn't feel like I was failing daily. Their grades needed to represent their achievement in comparison to where they were at the beginning of the year. I kept percentages of each score on their papers and tests and averaged them at the end of the week. Since I feel that success breeds success, I was aiming to make them aware of their accomplishments, while at the same time being as realistic as possible about where they were now and where they needed to be by the end of the year. Often I felt that goals never entered their minds, though we set them regularly.

The days in January were long and fairly productive. The children had just rested from the routine of school, so they welcomed it back and we began a wonderful rhythm of hard work. I looked forward to my plans to take the children to the beach in the spring, and as I talked with parents I laid the groundwork for their trusting me enough to take four children each weekend. I made out the permission slips and we began the process of planning to take the first group.

Chapter Twenty-One

The Beach

The second weekend in February turned out to be a beautiful one. Our first four students—Steadman, Mia, Tyrone, and Deasia—came with us out to the coast. My husband drove and we played games on the way after picking the children up at the school. I had checked my plans out with the principal, head teacher, and had the permission slips, signed by the parents in my folder.

Along with our discussion over Christmas break, another convincing factor in our decision to pursue these outings was a conversation that my husband had had with police patrolling the school area. He was originally thinking we could possibly have a picnic in the park with the children and their families toward the end of the year. This was something I had always tried to arrange with my other classrooms. The policeman said it was possible, but he'd have to add officers to help us, because the city parks in that area weren't safe. This was a discouraging fact, and so we decided to bag the idea of picnicking and just do our weekly trips to the Oregon coast with four students at a time.

As we got out of town, Tyrone said, "Wow, look at that

green field!" Living in the city, the children saw mostly concrete; they had encountered grass in yards, but never a full field of beautiful grass with hills in the background.

As we drove along, my husband said "O.K. Every car we pass belongs to one of us. We'll take turns claiming the car." It was fun and we laughed a lot as we found that the ugly cars went to my husband. They loved it!

He taught them to skip rocks over the creek behind a rest stop that we found halfway there. We stretched and walked and the children wanted to skip rocks over the water. The trick was to find the flat rocks and throw them at just the right angle. My husband was good at it, and the children learned quickly.

When we got to the shore we went to an aquarium. It was a great lesson in sea life and prepared us to head for the ocean beach next. Tyrone hesitated when we got to the beach. He had a deformed foot and was reluctant to take his shoes and socks off. My husband sat down with him and told his story. My husband was born with six toes on each foot. It was an anomaly in his family, because no one had had that happen before. It was unusual no matter where he went and he learned to not be embarrassed by it. He had two big toes. He quickly took his shoes and socks off and showed Tyrone how they looked.

Without any further hesitation, Tyrone threw off his shoes and socks and headed for the water. I waded out there as well, to make sure I could grab anyone who might venture out too far. We played in the sand and enjoyed the beautiful ocean scene. The sky was a brilliant blue that day, and the sand was warm, but the water, as usual, was icy cold. We built sand castles and covered our toes in the warmth of the sand.

It wasn't long until it was past lunchtime, so we hurried to a small hamburger shop where they allowed us to change clothes in the restroom and dust away the sand and dirt. We had a good lunch and made plans for the afternoon. There was an amusement center where they had bumper cars and nothing was more fun than to bump into your teacher's car. It was especially fun to bump into my husband's car, as he made loud noises, and they laughed and joked.

Later we went out to an abandoned ship that had wrecked on the shore years ago. We took pictures with our Polaroid camera and so they had a remembrance of the day to take home. The final leg of our trip was to drive to our house where I had prepared food to be put in the oven quickly and we had dinner together.

While I was preparing the meal, the children could roam around our backyard. We were renting a home at the time, and oddly enough it had a swimming pool. Though it was pretty cold to get into it in February, it was fun to dangle their feet there and catch a small frog that was by the pool. Of course they wanted to skip rocks across the pool.

Oddly enough, the house also had a small palm tree by the pool. The Pacific northwest doesn't usually have the climate to keep a palm tree alive. One of the stipulations we had when we signed the rental agreement was to care for the palm tree in the cool northwest. The owner of the property was pretty adamant about that, because it needed tender loving care to survive. It had to have insulation around it in the winter and be carefully groomed in the summer. It was pretty interesting to the children, and they could have stayed there for much longer than our time frame permitted. A palm tree was something most of them had not experienced before our trip.

It was time for supper, so we called them in and enjoyed our meal together. Our agreement was to have the children back to their homes by 8:00 p.m., so we headed to the inner city. The day had gone by quickly, but it was a day I hoped would stay in their minds forever! A day away from the city in the peace and tranquility of a small town, a beautiful ocean, and time with their teacher that didn't require work and challenges was worthwhile to them. I hoped that it was a time for a different kind of bonding than they had ever experienced before.

Bonding with children can happen through many avenues. One is in the classroom as they feel accepted, praised, and guided. I feel that children need to know that you care about them. Another way is at recess. Most teachers love the idea of not being on recess duty, but most of us admit that you learn about children watching them play, talking to them during their free times, and being available to them if they just want to stand beside you and talk. Depending on your personality, talks with children can be joking with them, responding in fun and laughing ways, or being available for quiet talks if they need some time.

We went to the beach six different times spanning three months. It was a delight to hear the children tell the next group how much fun they had. The expectations rose with each passing week. Some of the parents who had been reluctant to sign the permission slip finally, at the persistent pleas of their child, gave in to the pressure, and in the end every student experienced going to the beach with us. It's a fond memory for my husband and me, and we were happy to give our weekends to my students. We did this the next year as well, and we always thought of some celebration to do with my students either during or at the end of each year. As the year progresses, the students become like your own children, and we have so many happy memories of those fun-filled times.

Over the years I've talked to adults about what they remember from their grade school years. Many, to my amazement, remembered very little about what went on in their early school years. Knowing this, I will always wonder what my inner-city kids will have remembered about their year in my class. I'm thinking they probably won't forget this trip to the beach that we took. It was an escape for a day in the midst of a stressful life for them. They were excited and to a person seemed to enjoy this moment in time. Though they may forget many things, I hope they associated this year with a little bit of fun along with what I hoped was a worthwhile learning year for them! I know it is good advice to live in the moment. I was trying to do that along with my students.

Chapter Twenty-Two

Testing

The dreaded time had arrived. Neither teachers nor students looked forward to the testing days. The children were worried about doing their best on the writing exam. I was worried that a test day was just one day in the life of a child. What if it was a particularly bad day for them?

If the child didn't feel well or had a bad night or morning, there would be no way that they could test to the degree of expertise that was possible for them. I chose a Tuesday, Wednesday, and Thursday to complete the writing exam. Mondays they were usually tired, and this was true on Fridays as well. Most schools in which I taught suggested the days I chose.

On the writing exam, the students were given three choices of topics. On the first day they were to do their planning and make their outline. The second day was for writing and possibly editing as much as they could within the time frame. The final day they were to write in the booklet provided and write their final copy in ink. I chose erasable ink pens. Though they weren't ideal, the pens afforded them the opportunity to erase if they caught a misspelled word, punctuation error, or a poor word choice.

They were to read and re-read. This was something I emphasized as I taught writing throughout the year. Bringing it to a finished copy was tedious, but it certainly helped them to have practice throughout the year. For the most part I was pleased with their concentration level. Most of the students had learned that writing wasn't as bad as they thought, and it was a wonderful opportunity to express themselves on a variety of subjects.

Most of them needed to express their emotions—how they felt about life. At the end of Thursday, I picked up the writing composition booklets and put them directly into the manila envelope that was provided. I put the envelope directly into the hands of Ms. Lanikin. She was to send both fifth-grade classes' booklets to the state department and they wouldn't be returned until the end of the school year. Quick feedback wasn't possible in a statewide test, as teams of teachers who were trained to grade them assessed the writing. It was a hard job.

The next sets of test would come in March and April. They were the reading and math tests and we had a lot of work to do to complete our preparation for those very difficult exams. Basic skills were a problem, as the children from stressful homes had a hard time retaining the skills they learned. They rarely thought of school in the summer at all, and throughout the year, much review was needed just to keep children on track with remembering the necessary skills.

In my early teaching days, we used standardized tests as a diagnostic tool. We gave them in the fall to discover areas of need. We adapted our curriculum to those weaker areas and worked hard to improve them. We then re-tested at the end of the year to measure growth. I have always felt this is the best use of standardized tests. It helped both teachers and students.

Teaching is a very high level skill that needs constant monitoring. My experience over time proved that if you introduced a new concept, it would be retained best if it were reviewed within twenty-four hours. The first day it would only go into short-term memory, but as I re-taught, it would become more stable for long-term retention. So if I introduced a new math concept on Monday and reviewed it on Tuesday, the children's graph of learning would stay about the same. If I briefly reviewed it each day of that week and every other day of the following week, then again in three weeks, and in five, they would probably retain it … but there were no promises. It would have to be reviewed the following year after a summer of no studying.

You can imagine how important it was to keep track of the skills I was teaching my fifth graders. Once I introduced a math skill and reviewed it for a week, I turned the pages of my lesson plan book and wrote that skill in for three weeks later. I knew that the same math skills would be returned to as they entered middle school, but they also were expected to have a solid base of the skills that they learned in fifth and prior grades.

Homework, I always felt, helped children review the skills introduced and reinforce the schedule of learning I have outlined. I didn't send homework for any new skill until it had been reviewed several times. Sadly, it is often just an exercise in tedium for children. To be effective, homework must either promote retention of previous learning or challenge the mind to expand its thinking; ideally, homework should help children delight in discovery through reading an intriguing book or engaging in creative work.

Creative homework reaches more into the right side of the

brain, and involves subjects such as art, music, and writing. For example: "Thinking about the word, 'catastrophe,' illustrate and write a comment about what pictures this word brings into your mind." This would certainly be more engaging than saying, "Using your dictionary, write the definition of 'catastrophe.'"

Practice homework is important as well. If I have taught and reviewed adding fractions, I would want to send a homework page that reinforces the practice and helps its retention.

In most cases parents in busy households would prefer that assigned work at home not be so difficult that the child can't accomplish it alone. A teacher would like cooperation from parents in making sure there is a time set aside specifically for their children to sit down each night and work a short while. With some students, maintaining a time right after school works best for them. For others, it would be better just before bedtime. Some teachers and parents prefer homework packets, parceled out over time so that homework isn't a nightly necessity. I prefer giving shorter assignments every night, because it establishes a habit that becomes ingrained in children as they move through their educational careers.

I tried to visit with parents about what worked best for them as well as what would be best for the students. Parent-teacher cooperation on this is essential to making homework improve children's learning. The task shouldn't be dreaded or defamed at home. It's wonderful if parents monitor it, but that doesn't always happen. I believe that a reasonable amount of homework is effective, but if it takes all evening to complete, it becomes counterproductive.

Chapter Twenty-Three

Problems

The phone rang in my classroom, which was a little unusual. I answered, and the principal's voice rang through the line: Lock the door immediately!"

I ran to the door and threw the lock shut just in time, because someone was pounding on the door.

"I'm taking Steadman home! Let me in this room." The children looked at me as the pounding continued. "Open this door! I know you are in there."

We all sat looking at each other. I was totally perplexed. I had what I thought was a good relationship with Steadman's mother. I had such admiration for this young man. I felt that his mother had become a little more positive toward her son and the school. Part of me wanted to let her in and try to speak to her, but I knew I had no choice but to obey the principal who had given me the command. Perhaps I would find out later what caused her to give me the direction to not open the door.

Steadman had his head on the desk, and I was so very sad that he was feeling humiliated and upset. He didn't move to talk to me, nor did he say anything to anyone around him. He certainly didn't respond to his mother who was shouting for him to come out the door. In fact my students were extremely quiet—unusually so. She knocked for a few minutes, determined to make her demands. We all sat quietly waiting for her to leave. There was no security in our building, so the only recourse was to wait and not open the door.

As the knocking subsided, I returned to our normal workday. The children never asked, nor did I, about the interruption. The principal didn't explain her actions and I never really knew what caused this interlude in our day. Perhaps it was better not to know. Later I heard it had to do with something that happened in an after-school program, but that was merely speculation.

Work continued but spring fever was about to descend upon our year. It is always more difficult to keep children focused as good weather enters the picture. I watched the neighborhood begin to get louder. People stood on street corners talking in larger groups than they had during the winter months, and possible problems could be developing with every group. The gang activity in the neighborhood began to heat up; I was getting nervous for the safety of the children. My fifth graders were easy bait as potential gang members. Their peer groups and those of their older brothers and sisters easily influenced them, so keeping them safe became a priority for me.

I called the DARE officer whom I had worked with in the fall of the year. We talked about what was happening in the neighborhood, and I asked if he could pay another visit to my classroom to see if he could review the steps it takes to avoid peer pressure. I certainly thought he would have an impact on my students. We set up a date for the following Friday morning. The students looked forward to seeing him again and he spent time with them in the classroom and on the playground at recess time. Did it help? I don't know. That is often the case with my career. The results of what you do are not easily apparent. I would never know who joined gangs from that point on, or what my influence had been in the long term.

Our trips to the beach had ended and my husband and I wanted to spend some time with the most vulnerable students to make sure they had something to do over the weekend. We gathered four of them that Saturday and got written permission to take them to a new movie we thought they'd like to see. After a treat following the movie, we took them home only to find yellow tape in the middle of the block where we were returning Tyrone.

Someone had been shot in that neighborhood, and we were escorted to and from his house by a policeman. His house was just barely inside the area cordoned off for police work, so he was able to go home. My husband and I looked at each other in dismay. We made sure Tyrone's mother was home before departing, but it still wasn't easy to walk away, knowing he was back there.

My concern was to make each day as productive as I could. My assignment was amazingly difficult. Those students who were struggling were losing some of their reserve energy due to late nights, hot days, and lack of incentive from all of the right places. Mikayle hadn't been in school for a while and the rumor was that she finally got to go stay with her mother, who lived in another part of the neighborhood. I was hoping a new environment would keep her off the streets and help her to be happy and more adjusted to school. I never knew what happened in the end, though I still think of her often.

Chapter Twenty-Four

The Staff, Again

We were into negotiations. Salary issues were always a part of the discussions during a contract negotiation year. Some contracts over the course of my career were set up on a three-year basis; others were two- or even one-year contracts. This depended on how difficult it was to come to agreement on health insurance and salaries. Levies had to be passed in order to appropriate funding in some years, depending on the state funds available. The levies were for "extra" money to meet budgets. The money came from property tax in most cases, until tax limitations were voted into law. Often we received unfunded mandates from the State Department of Education. For example, if the state required us to have a full-time aide to assist an autistic child, it often was not funded but needed to be taken into consideration for the budget. Since my husband was a superintendent of schools, I could easily see the administration's concerns as well as the teachers' point of view. It always made me uncomfortable to be in negotiations.

It is pretty well agreed that teachers are underpaid for their efforts. I began my career in 1960 with a contract in a small town in Montana. I received $2500 for the year. We paid $35 a month for our apartment, which was part of a teacher residence owned by the school. We didn't have to pay for three months, because we didn't get paid in the summer. It was tricky to budget and live on that salary, even though my husband made $3200 because he also had coaching duties. By the time I was teaching at the Rosa Parks School, I had twenty years of experience and a masters' degree in education, and I was still being paid in the $30,000 range. We always worked hard to keep our personal budget in line.

Big issues in education over time have included the idea of merit pay. I have never been in favor of it. The market place is competitive by its very nature; I think the opposite should be true in a school setting. Cooperation among all staff members is so important to the overall success of the students. I believe in cooperative work to better a school. Most teachers I worked with worked as hard as they could and endeavored to improve their skills by attending workshops, participating in in-house training sessions, and reading everything they could to be the best possible in their teaching. Teachers get into the profession because they want to help children. I am not naïve enough to think that every teacher does this, but I feel the large majority of them care deeply and work hard.

Merit pay by definition would elevate certain teachers and judge them superior to others. It might limit what teachers share about their methods and their teaching techniques with each other. It would force teachers to spend more time on teaching to a test that would limit creativity and excitement for children. I know teachers and education should be better funded than they are presently, but instead of going toward merit pay, that money could go toward professional workshops and other areas of need.

Being in negotiations meant meetings after school occasionally to hear reports on the progress from the negotiating committee. My colleagues were upset that the administration seemed to be unwilling to move closer to the teachers' proposals. I could feel emotions rising and knew that many of my colleagues were edging toward strike mentality. As I sat there, I thought of how easy it would be to join them in their thinking. Certainly as many hours as I was working, coupled with the amount of books and supplies I bought over the year, should be somehow compensated. Then again, I knew that schools had to operate within a budget. Luckily, that spring, things were ironed out and all was settled. It was with a sigh of relief that we signed our contracts for the next year.

Many staff committees were forming at that time to make plans for the next year. I could hardly believe the year was coming to a close. I was put on a committee with Bill, the P.E. teacher. We actually began to communicate, and I enjoyed his insight and point of view on the issues that were most important to all of us. He had been on this staff for many years, while I was just ending one year, so I listened and soaked up any knowledge I could that would move me closer to being accepted across color lines. I felt more comfortable and at ease as we sat discussing problems and solutions for the coming year.

Maybe his earlier reluctance to spend time with me stemmed from his experiences. Perhaps he saw many white teachers come and go, though there were several on staff. His personality was stoic, I knew, so I was happy he at last began to communicate with me. He never really joined into casual talk; I never saw him in the teachers' staff area, as he had the lunchroom duty. Still, I enjoyed getting to know him; he was an interesting personality.

Chapter Twenty-Five

Field Trips

One of the most intriguing field trips for the fifth graders was always their trip to middle school to check out next year's venue. Many were worried about understanding how to do the combination for their lockers. Others were sure that they wouldn't like the school, the teachers, and especially the unfamiliar environment. I tried reassuring them on all counts. This middle school chose to have the students shadow a sixth grader to get a little familiar with how middle school felt. The students each received a letter from the person they would shadow, giving them advice about how to ease their way into middle school life. The day was productive and well organized by the staff at the middle school. The children were so excited about their advancement to sixth grade, but they were more excited to be able to change classrooms and be a part of the middle-school scene.

Other field trips we took were fun for me as well. We went to the Science Center a couple of times during the year. The OMNIMAX Theatre had just been built at the center and was a new experience for all of us. The first movie

I chose was about the Blue Angels. I was so impressed by the discipline it took for pilots to become a part of this elite group. They lived, breathed, studied, and practiced to achieve the quality of expertise necessary to achieve such advanced piloting skills. We discussed how their daily life went, and how their example could help all of us achieve the degree of expertise we wanted in any field of endeavor. I especially wanted my students to apply that level of discipline to their studying, their homework, and their daily attention in class. Maybe it would serve as an inspiration to someone along the way.

The first trip to the center was so much fun that I studied the theatre schedule and found that we had just enough money to attend one more session. There was a movie about beavers that I thought would make a good science unit. We studied every aspect of their lives, their work, and the industrious nature of their daily schedule. We built small beaver dams, made beaver characters, and at last attended the film as the culmination of our unit. I hope that it helped the students appreciate nature study and inspired them to keep reading about other animals. They certainly seemed to engage in the story of the beaver family we viewed on film. Plus, getting to take a field trip was a great relief after the state math and reading tests. I was happy to have a change of pace with the students as well and to offer a little fun with the ending school projects.

Chapter Twenty-Six

Graduation

It was nearing the end of the school year, and I was told about the plans for a graduation ceremony to launch our fifth graders onto middle school. It was quite an elaborate program. Music, speeches, awards, and of course diplomas were all a part of this special day. The students were excited about every part of it, and since it was my first year, I was an avid observer of the school's traditions.

Every child was to dress up to receive his/her diploma and to take part in the ceremony. I was excited for them. We gathered in our classrooms and started to line up to march over to the gymnasium. I looked back at the line with a sigh. Though the year showed many achievements, walking in a straight line wasn't one of them. No matter how much I practiced with them, it was not worth the time and effort, because the children simply did not fall into lock step like most students. They ambled along, talking and gesturing excitedly, not at all aware of my despair at the sloppiness of our entry into the building. However, their performance at graduation was perfect. They were attentive, interested, proud of their achievements, and eager for the cake and punch that followed the festivities.

Report cards were handed out to students along with their diplomas and I was proud to be told by the principal that the children's writing scores had jumped much higher than expected. Inside I rejoiced. Many hard days of writing instruction and practice were vindicated. The children received copies of their writing tests. I could feel their pride and felt like it was a gift they could take with them forever as they kept honing their skills. As I said goodbyes and gave hugs, a few tears came to my eyes. I knew these children were going on to the rest of their lives, and I was glad to have been a small part of their accomplishments.

From the beginning of the year to now was a world of difference. My children smiled more, were more earnest in their approach to learning, and seemed excited about the prospects of middle school.

Steadman became a dedicated student, earnest in his questions and excited about the top grades he received. Mia was looking like a sixth grader in demeanor and maturity. She would be successful, I thought as I gave her a hug, and I told her so. Deasia was taller than I and very shy as she handed me a gift. Her grandmother had graciously allowed her to pick out a necklace for me as a thank you. I was very touched and grateful. Ebony had become so much more mature as she faced the challenges of her attention deficit problems. She knew she had had a good year and she was most proud of her report card. Tyrone was happy that not only were his grades better, but he also had not gotten into a fight since the middle of the year. This was an amazing change for him, and we rejoiced together as he showed me his diploma.

I couldn't change everything about their world, of course. While we celebrated, there was quite a commotion outside. Apparently two ladies got into a fistfight over their mutual boyfriend, who was just getting out of prison, I was told. I sighed with sadness at how tempers can flare and problems dim the beauty of a special day.

Chapter Twenty-Seven

The End of a Year

I went back to school for the end-of-the-year clean up. The children helped to scrub desks, put away books, and pack their possessions. I knew they were headed for summer break, so they were excited. Goodbyes were special but always sad.

I also began to plan for my next year. The principal and I had talked about moving the fifth-grade classrooms into the school. I requested it, as I felt that it would lend some support to the students and allow us to feel more a part of the general student body.

We made other plans for the next year as I moved to my new classroom. The room was going to be used to teach summer school, so I was able to prepare it for a new teacher to step in for a while. It looked like an exciting curriculum for the summer and they were moving an opossum in a cage into the class. I was surprised by its size and amazed at where they got it and how they could keep it there for any length of time.

As I sat at my desk after all was done for the year, I thought about a teacher's plight. We never know how the student turns out in the end. Our success is purely speculative. We do things that seem to work, and some that don't. I thought about the time that I had a young fifth grader in my class. I had previously had his older sister and older brother, both of whom had quit school. I was worried about Jimmy because he was headed in the same direction. Reading was especially difficult for him. How could I change the influence of his family history?

That year my class pets had been guinea pigs. They are cute little creatures that are furry and gentle. I use to love being greeted by their squeaky chatter as I walked into the class in the morning. They were asking me to feed them, because they were quite hungry, but I took it as a friendly greeting. The children loved them, and Jimmy especially was excited about the guinea pigs. He wanted to learn more about them, so I got him a little book that can be found in most pet stores full of facts about guinea pigs. I knew that reading it would be hard for him, but maybe this would just be the incentive he needed to see the value of reading.

He read and re-read that book about guinea pigs until it was tattered and worn. It made me happy to see it. He decided he wanted to raise some of his own, and he got a male and female and began to set up his business at home for his project. Sure enough, guinea pigs were bred and born, and he sold them for a profit. I noticed that as he learned to read the guinea pig book, he also transferred that love of reading to other books.

I always wanted to know if he stayed in school and graduated—the first in his family. The satisfaction a teacher feels for seeing results is wonderful. I would love to be able to hear about all of the students I nurtured during my career, but unfortunately I moved to new places, and the results of my labor were never apparent to me. Still, each year brought me pleasure and excitement, and I relished the joy of watching children grow and learn.

I tried to concentrate on the successes of the year. I thought of the children who finally started to smile. I remembered how they grew and changed throughout the year. There were the ones who finally felt comfortable about raising their hands and answering questions. How exciting those "ah-ha!" moments are to a teacher. We love them; we store them in our hearts; they are what propel us to the next year.

I taught in this inner-city school for one more year. Sadly I wasn't able to continue my commute there, as my husband retired and we moved out of the range for a reasonable drive to the city. I continued to teach for four more years in a school near our new home. After that I helped for two years part time with the Title I reading program, and then I helped administer a grant in that school that provided support to the whole school reading program. I loved my position and hopefully helped other teachers and students by dedicating my time to the entire school. I am presently retired, but the teachers, principals, and superintendents of the schools where I worked—and, honestly, of most schools across our country—remain dedicated and caring educators.

I have, however, yearned to tell the story of my experience in the inner city. Would the color lines dissolve, as did the prejudices about different religions and nationalities from previous times? My hope is that schools and parents help eliminate such divisive thought early. Our potential is only limited by our hesitance in reaching out and mastering our goals. Can prejudice go away, or do we as a nation accept one segment of society and not another? Do we transfer prejudice in waves of public opinion? I hope not!

Racial issues are still around after decades of some

people wanting to erase the lines that divide us culturally and racially. Why? I saw those lines and felt them keeping me from truly getting to know some of the staff members. I hoped that no one in the school ever felt any rejections from me, because it was a part of my very core to accept, to try to understand, and to seek to dissolve those barriers. I have included in my last chapter many of the changes that I felt were of major importance in achieving all-school success.

How important is elementary education? I think it is immensely crucial to the successful raising of our children. Early signs of absence, neglect, hunger, and abuse can be caught and changed with careful analysis. Some have said these early signs give us the opportunity to change a child's success level in so many ways, perhaps even keep them from a life of crime. Tremendous caring on the part of a teacher can move mountains in the child's life. That's why I have loved my profession and enjoyed the challenge of making each child's life more hopeful, secure, and successful. Success breeds success, while the opposite scenario predicts a life less happy and less productive.

As I analyzed what worked well in educational practice, I thought about how we in education at times have thrown away good teaching practices to embrace some new, untried ideas. I believe we should consider everything we do in the classroom in order to choose wisely. We don't have a minute to waste. Using research and our own experiences, we need to fine-tune our skills and share ideas for the betterment of all members of the school community.

The world of schools and education is an amazing one, and I am always excited to hear about someone else's plans for promoting curriculum, helping a child, and encouraging success. Teachers for the most part are highly creative and motivated to help all students. After all, the school year at Rosa Parks had barely ended, and I was already making plans for next year! I knew the challenges would be immense with the new students who awaited me. The heart of a teacher is big, full of tears of joy and sorrow. My heart was ready for the next adventure.

Epilogue

I have highlighted and emphasized some of the following points as vital to a successful school.

1. An active school principal, who works well with the staff, listens to them, hears their needs, and praises their successes, will promote longevity of staff members in his or her building. Longevity is important to building a successful school program.

2. Collegiality among teachers—sharing ideas, working together, and setting shared goals—is paramount to success. There must be a program for mentoring new teachers by linking each with a staff member. Cultural differences and activities common to the school environment should be taught to new teachers, perhaps by staff members from a different race or teaching a different grade level. This would help everyone to get to know faculty and staff at all levels.

3. Parent involvement and cooperation with the teachers is vital. Teachers must call parents, get acquainted with them early in the year. E-mail and computer information is great, but speaking directly to them is more personal. They are the teachers' best partners.

4. Proper funding of essential materials must be found. Administrators need to work with and listen to teachers about what materials are vital. As much as

administrators can, they should be present in the classroom and staff room to hear needs, learn what works, and encourage sharing that will make for a strong school.

5. It is important to emphasize needed breaks for children and teaching them to solve inter-relationship problems they encounter on the playground and in the classroom. Give all children time to express themselves. Listen to them.

6. Success cannot be based solely on standardized tests. Tests are a day in the life of a child. Success can be seen by attitudes, completed assignments, improved behavior and grades that show progress.

7. Have strong methods for teaching *all* subject areas, highlighting the achievement and excitement of learning necessary for math and science. These two subjects seem to be in great need in our country. Retain your best ideas and add new ones as you progress.

8. Expressing themselves through their writing is such an important gift to give children. Teach them to write their feelings, their ideas, their hopes, fears, and their goals in life.

9. Think out of the box in grouping children. Ability grouping has been around for a long time. It segregates children and is often uninspiring. Always put the students' feelings about themselves paramount in any decision. Success breeds success.

10. Know the principles of learning. Study what helps children retain information, solve problems, grow and change, and become self-motivating. Attend all possible workshops and classes to keep improving skills. Share ideas with all staff members who seek your advice.

Bibliography

Books

Glad well, Malcolm. <u>The Outliers</u>, Little, Brown and Co: Hachette Book Group, New York, N.Y., 2008.

Hunter, Madeline. <u>Mastery Teaching,</u> El Segundo, CA: TIP Publication, 1982, 1986, and 1994.

Hunter, Madeline. <u>Formulating Lesson Plans, The Madeline Hunter Direct Instruction Model.</u> El Segundo: CA TIP Publication, 1982, 1986, and 1994.

Hunter, Madeline. <u>Enhancing Teaching,</u> El Segundo, and Ca: TIP Publication, 1982, 1986. 1994, 1996.

Kohn, Alfie. <u>Punishing By Rewards,</u> The Trouble With Gold Stars, Incentive Plans, A's, Praise and Other Bribes. Boston: Houghton Mifflin, 1993/1999.

Newpapers and Magazines

Park, Alice. "The Long-Term Effects of Spanking," <u>Time</u> Magazine, May 3, 2010.

Large, Jerry. "Unconscious Bias is Real Challenge." The Seattle Times. July,2010

Internet

Bendtro, Larry K. Phd. "From Coercive to Strength—Based Intervention: Responding to the Needs of Children in Pain. January, 2004.

Boddy-Evans, Marion. Right Brain/Left Brain: What Is It All About? http://painting.about.com/od/right left brain/a/right-Brain.htm. 11/19/09

Brooks, David, "The Quiet Revolution, "New York Times Op-Ed. 10/22/2009

Cairney, Trevor. The 4th R: Rest! "Literacy, Families and Learning," http://trevorcairney.blogspot.com/2009/03/4th-r-rest.html. 3/11/2009.

Inner City Schooling. University of Michigan. http://sitemaker.umich.edu/mitchellyellin.356/parental-involvement.

Little, Judith Warren. "Norms of Collegiality and Experimentation: Workplace Conditions of School Success!" http://aer.sage.pub.com/cgi/content/short/19/3/325. "American Research Journal, "11/18/09.

KWANZAA. The first Fruit Celebration. www.afrocentricnews.com/html/kwanza.htm.

Parker-Pope, Tara, "The 3 R's? A Fourth Is Crucial, Too: Recess. "New York Times," www.nytimes.com/2009/02/24/hearth,24well.html?--r=1.2/23/2009.

Pop ham, James W. "Standardized Testing Fails the Exam. http://www.edutopia.org/f-for-assessment.

Poulton, Shirley. Power Writing Plus:Teach the Traits of Effective Writing. Grand Haven MI:C&C Graphics Publication, 2004. http://www.thewritingsite.org.

"Reflecting on Longevity," Perimeter Primate. Perimeterprimate.blogspot.com/2009/01/call-for-longevity. html.

Sheer, Michael D., Anderson, Nick. "President Obama Discusses New "Race to the Top" Program. Washington Post. http://www.washingtonpost.com/wp-dyn/content/article/2009/07/23/AR20009072302938.html?sid=ST200 9072303922.7/23/2009 5:29 PM.

"Sleep is the Right Ingredient for Academic Success," www. sciencedaily.com.8/02/07.

Stolberg, Sheryl Gay. "Obama Puts Spotlight on Education Grants." The Caucus Blog—New York Times. 11/16/09.

White, Johyn. Secretary Duncan Sets Tone for "Race to the Top" Ed.gov. US Department of Education. 5/19/2009.

Whitehurst, Grover J. "Russ," Croft, Michello. "Faith in Common Standards Not Enough." Blog http://www. brookings.edu/opinions/2009, 1029-standards-whitehurst. aspx.